PLAYING WITH BLOCKS

THE REINNOVATION OF HIGH SCHOOL

WILLIAM G. CLOO ED.D.

Playing with Blocks
The Reinnovation of High School

ISBN   978-1-7375745-1-4 (print)
            978-1-7375745-0-7 (ebook)

To learn more about consulting and speaking engagements, email Dr. Cloo at PlayingWithBlocks2021@gmail.com

PlayingWithBlocks2021.com
Facebook: PlayingWithBlocks2021
Instagram: @PlayingWithBlocks2021

Book design by StoriesToTellBooks.com

To my friend and neighbor, Joe Pope, who is the impetus for the writing.

To my mentors: Dr. Marilou Ryder, Dr. Jonathan Greenberg, Dr. Marilyn Saucedo, Dr. Reggie Thompkins, and Dr. Kristi Coulter, who advised and motivated me along the way.

To my wife, the rock that grounds me and the water that allows me to grow.

To my Grandma, Phyllis Onken, who never inhibited my ideas and inspired me to continue to create.

Foreword

On August 29, 2020, my friend Joe and I were watching our favorite football team, Liverpool, compete for the Community Cup, which they did not attain. This was one of many times in our lives when we communed under the same banner for a common purpose and to get a respite from life. This particular time was new, however. This was the first time we were in close proximity (within six feet, masks on) in more than four months. COVID-19 had devastated the world, particularly, the United States. Voluntary isolation was the norm, whether you had the disease or not. My mother was ailing and was a patient in a residential facility. I had not been allowed to see her in over six months. The turbulent political atmosphere was at a fever pitch. The elections were in full rhetorical exchange in a climate of high racial tension. Regardless of where in the spectrum anyone was, the anxiety and tension were palpable, day after day after day. People were dying, people were demonstrating, people were arguing … people were uncertain.

One subject in front of every family was the backlash of COVID-19 shelter-at-home orders on education. Parents wanted, and needed, to go back to work, but the environment was not safe. School districts had moved their structure to online learning and were using the computer as the main method of educating. Learning platforms that had been used for years by colleges had to be adapted for younger audiences. This one aspect put a lot of pressure on the creativity of the classroom teacher. Although the training levels varied, teachers did not have the necessary preparation to handle this process. Most importantly, the educational system was not prepared to adopt a new model, given the current perspectives and visions it currently held.

As a current teacher and recent administrator, I struggled with many educational aspects during this time. For two years I had declared a sabbatical from administration to create an opportunity to complete my Ed.D. in Organizational Leadership from Brandman University. Little did I know that the world we knew would require transformation. Few leaders—or anyone else, for that matter—foresaw it. So I sat in my dining room every day, changing the delivery of educational content in new ways for my students and holding my tongue from an organizational standpoint on what the educational system should do. I knew this was a prime opportunity for school districts to innovate all aspects of the educational system in a way that could really benefit all communities. The big question was how.

Sitting on the couch in my friend's living room, Joe and I exchanged ideas about our current situations. We are in different places on the political pendulum but have always been able to exchange ideas and focus on the advancement of our society. We naturally tend to debate ideas and not ideologies because vision and compromise keep society advancing. Joe is in management and shared the different changes and outlooks of his business in adapting to the COVID-19 pandemic. It was at that moment that my world changed. Joe started asking how education was going to work on becoming better for kids. He specifically addressed class size and wondered if the teacher/student ratio would change. He recalled his college days when some classes were hundreds deep with only one teacher, and he wondered why high schools couldn't have that model. It was there, trying to explain the current system, when an idea formed into something unique. Why couldn't Joe's idea happen? The tenured teacher in me automatically thought of the overworked and the massive number of people unemployed, yet the organizational leader in me thought my friend might be onto something. As I pondered on the situation further after my team's heartbreaking loss—not too hard, they were Premier champions—I couldn't shake the philosophy of utilizing personnel for their talent expertise, a concept made famous by the movie *Moneyball*. What if we restructured the educational team to contribute their best assets to the game of learning? It is from there that this book was started and the journey to a new vision began.

Introduction

There is a room in our house that is designated as a children's playroom. For years, children of our family and friends have utilized this room for fun and games, which has produced memories that have lasted a lifetime. From tea parties to airplane battles to coloring sessions, this room has housed many different inventive outlets for children. In reflecting on the current state of education, I was reminded of a key thing that would occur in this room. I was fascinated with how kids, in early ages, played with blocks. These simple, inexpensive items produced a world of creative expression and sociology I never before experienced. Some of the occurrences helped conceptualize the innovations outlined in this book.

When my nieces and nephews were younger, they would play in the playroom, with my wife and I observing and interacting. It was thoroughly amazing to see the type of person each youngster was at that age. Each person built their unique structure. One child was focused on making the strongest structure and would barter for the best blocks. One child would want to lay out the entire town all over the floor and make sure everyone had an equal number of blocks. Another child was consumed with the aesthetics of building and the use of different colors. Then there was that child who loved to conquer the other castles and lay siege on the people. These interactions were a testing ground of cooperation, collaboration, and conflict resolution.

One key thing I noticed was that when the one child would destroy the castles, the others would express their disappointment and then immediately start the game over again. They did not just start rebuilding the same structure but would start the bartering and conceptual phase all over again. Each child would want to make the next structure better than the previous one. The kids would talk about the old castle and its weaknesses. They would look at each block and evaluate its strengths and weaknesses. Sometimes, they would ask to redesign the current block with statements like, "Is there a block with a round top, flat and round?" The purpose was to find the best pieces for their new structure. They would trade and negotiate with the limited blocks in the room so that all had a somewhat fair amount. Then the reconstruction would begin, with some structures being completely different. Other structures were erected similar to the previous but with modifications that made it better.

The children would eventually achieve the goal of the best possible structure, which meant that the game would be over (for the time being) and a new game was needed. In the end, the structures were never able to withstand the monster that was 50 times the size of the structure, and the kids always had fun with destruction time just prior to clean up time.

This story about kids is the impetus for the opportunity before all educators. Thinking about their process now, I realized it is with this attitude that our educational system can be reborn.

The school system is a long-standing structure that has been analyzed and only changed in small ways since the Industrial Revolution. Each block of the structure is a segment of the school community. From the facilities to the job description of the employees, each component has an overall purpose that makes the school function. It is a strong structure with many rooms. COVID-19 is the first big destroyer to annihilate the school system, and the results will be long lasting. COVID is the monster 50 times bigger than the castle that toppled every element and scattered it all over the floor.

One of the many lessons from COVID has been the need for children to continue to learn at the best possible rate in order for society to continue. It seems to be the belief that society will be all right if children, who represent our future, continue to evolve. So as America slowly comes out of this pandemic, the educational system has a duty to rebuild the educational structure.

The metaphoric blocks of education are all over the floor. We must take a lesson from our children. We must re-envision school. We must look at each block and modify it if necessary. We must rebuild a new school that better serves all students in the new vision, based on current elements. While all levels of the education system—elementary, middle school, junior high, and high school—need restructuring, this book focuses only on my ideas for restructuring the high school system.

How to Read the Book

Leadership meetings are a time of collaboration and idea generation. However, most meetings are constrained to the immediate crises that plague the school site or district. Within those meetings, I was the type of person who would always ask the presenter questions. Yes. I was *that* guy. The one who would frequently start the exchange with, "What if …?" Throughout the years, I have been teased with groans and laughter for being the one who would not let things go until I was satisfied with the result. As an educational leader, I would always strive to flesh out the best ideas for the complete understanding of everyone to make sure we all progressed in the best way possible. I know my ideas were not necessarily welcomed at the outset, and I always sought feedback to make them better. I demanded that the results of the programs and events be as seamless as possible to best benefit the students.

It is in this spirit that I submit these humble offerings to the reader. These ideas are innovation starters for the leaders of our educational system to consider as we begin—and continue—the transition back to educating kids. By no means are these innovations meant to be the sole understanding of the "plug and play" concept. This is not a program but the beginning of a hard conversation that many leadership groups are hesitant to engage in with their teams.

The assumption of the traditional day schedule in high school is a six-period day, with central purpose being the requirements for graduation. A school needs to provide the opportunity for students to access a college later in life; however, the school's primary purpose is to ensure that state standards are met, and the students meet the high school requirements for matriculation. For years now, the slow denigration of the central purpose has occurred through manipulation by political aspirations and special interest forces within the educational environment. The educational system must regain a central focus to effectively teach students in order to meet its primary goal: the high school diploma. This is the prime directive of every school, and it must be the central focus of all things.

Each state, district, and school site is different, so it is expected that some things will not work for your stakeholders. That is okay. Each idea offered should be reviewed through the educational code and bylaws of your respective state and district. There might be the need for amendments and proposals to be passed by school boards in order to implement some of these measures. Teachers' unions must be consulted and kept in the fold. One thing I will guarantee with this book is that many ideas provided here will be disregarded, ignored, or argued because change is hard work—and sometimes, scary. The most important thing is to review your current process to make it better. We must look at the educational structure that has been implemented and consider building a new one, and if we build a better one, good on us. Some may take a portion of these ideas and create an even better system for their community. Awesome. The central purpose of this book is for leaders to honestly evaluate their current approaches to education, focus on their prime directives, and deliver the best education for students, not staff.

Change initiatives must start with ideas that seem radical when they are first proposed to the populace, and the ideas offered here are no exception. Steve Jobs, Thomas Edison, and Albert Einstein were each considered crazy at some point. Some measures outlined in this book will not be taken well by society because education has been the safety net to deal with society's problems. Parents will not like the outlined measures because the schools will no longer babysit their children until they are eighteen. Businesses will not like the aforementioned information because they will have to train their own workforces instead of trusting the schools to do it. Additionally, there will be a very large workforce that will be available for work at entry level jobs which are not available at this time. Local communities will find difficulties with these new measures because policing must occur twenty-four hours a day instead of only at night when children are out of school. So why read the book?

The educational community must regain its structural integrity and be willing to advocate wholeheartedly against the litigious process along with political institutions threatening funding. At the end of the day, everyone says that the children are our future and that we need to provide everything we possibly can for them. Yet— in back rooms that people don't like to talk about—the major focus shifts from the purpose of the school to the short-term political purpose the schools can provide. So, given these current elements within the landscape of the educational institutional process, we humbly offer an innovative structure that keeps the central focus of high school graduation as its centerpiece and all structures then revolving around that core.

Section 1

The Old Building

"Each person built their unique structure."

Chapter 1

The Life of a Teacher

Obviously, the life of a teacher is different depending on the grade level they teach. No level is better or harder than another; each just has different foci and needs. This book is focused on high school because of my experiences. However, this could well be adapted to an elementary understanding, with vision and extended innovation by a school's leaders.

Before COVID-19, each teacher's day began with a whirlwind of information and feedback and continued at an energetic pace until the final collapse at that last bell. On any given day, the teacher is expected to have:

◊ Prepared their lesson plan for the day
◊ Confirmed alignment with the standards
◊ Confirmed that any assessment (formative or summative) aligns with lesson, standards and pacing
◊ Created an agenda that provides engagement and newness while maintaining routine for their students
◊ Prepared the information throughout the room in engaging and visually appealing ways
◊ Cross referenced the needed materials for the day and ascertained they are available
◊ Received directives and announcements from students, parents, fellow teachers and district administration
◊ Confirmed technology is working or troubleshoot any problems

It's now 8:00 a.m. and the first period is about to start.

Following this time is the hurricane of exchange that each teacher maintains in educating children. They build and maintain relationships while dealing with student trauma or drama. Instructors present and justify educational input to students who would rather view their social media feeds.

Teachers entreat responses and feedback from students and adapt the lesson based on the responses. Teachers maintain an effective learning environment amid impulsive individuals who seek attention over knowledge. They consistently provide equity to students in a range from advance placement to special needs. Each element could be a full-time job in its own right.

Oh! And don't forget to be upbeat and smile!

These tasks do not even scratch the surface of the educator's daily experiences, given the multitudes of reactions and tragedies that are offered to the teacher. I will not even describe the second guessing, opinions, excuses, and accusations teachers receive from parents and administrators. OR the mountain of "Monday Morning Quarterbacks" who examine the most minuscule aspect of the learning process and extrapolate it to a cultural norm which must be addressed by the instructor alone. Most of these daily expectations are magnified by the current situation, given that the learning environment is now a collection of pictures and letters in circles (virtual meeting backgrounds), which limits the ability to monitor and enforce. Yet the responsibilities are still the same.

A gap in the current daily educational system is that teachers are not given the opportunity to truly influence their talents in a larger role. So many of these individuals are not supported as professionals to contribute to the school or district community during their school hours. These teachers must make a choice to either add even more work after their designated times (with little or no compensation) or spend time with their families and taking care of other aspects of their lives.

The current hierarchical structure creates a competitive environment for power. The result is, generally, bitterness and jealousy. It is no wonder why schools have challenges filling leadership roles within a school site; the demands of new roles on overworked teachers make it easier for these intelligent leaders to stay hidden and not even be noticed. How ironic that schools publicize the achievements of sports leadership for the district but not the academic achievements of their staff that directly affect the outcomes of the students. The current situation is that district personnel— being the sole decision makers—select classroom learning in consultation with publishers and only a small amount of opinion from teachers. This situation does not generate enough collective commitment for the maximization of committed funds.

The culminating product is a bunch of overworked people who desperately try to balance a life that is overwhelmingly focused on their careers. These people are taken advantage of because their hearts are enthralled with a desire to help kids. Eventually, fatigue plagues teachers to either lower their energy for work or remain overwhelmed. Both of these situations result in ineffective teaching.

Chapter 2

Education in Society

E ducation was specifically set up in order to give every citizen the basics to be successful in life. The understanding of reading and writing has been crucial to our civilization since the 1900s. Without these basic tools and skills, citizens would not be able to live up to what Jefferson referred to as the "informed citizenry" of the United States. The understanding of mathematics is not only necessary for people advancing to college, but it is also helpful to chefs and cooks and for those who measure, build, and create.

These requirements have not changed in any significant way. The needs for mathematical computation and algorithm creation have continued through the Information Age. Obviously, the necessity of being able to communicate in the written word is more valuable now than ever. Society sees the need for more inclusive academic language through the normalization of social media. Kids now use acronyms, contractions, and pictures to communicate for themselves what used to be communicated through the written word. Intention, tone, and a common basis for metaphor have been changed in such a fashion as to make miscommunication the biggest problem of our society.

Social media's algorithmic process of feeding United States cit-izens with only the things that would support them, along with adding an element of emergency, has done nothing but divide our country. It has made a life of complete misunderstanding of and non-agreement with the realities of any situation. Because people cannot agree on a common set of factors, citizens will never be able to compromise or find avenues of togetherness. It is not that one person is right or another person is wrong but that there is no agreed-upon set of factors and facts in place for people to make a conscientious compromise. It is these advanced levels of thinking that the high school level of education needs to address.

Education during the Industrial Age was focused on making sure people could survive in and contribute to a factory-oriented, industrialized nation. All aspects of education were focused on how they could participate in capitalism. The Information Age has changed that concept, so people automatically responded by thinking that college was the pathway to success. Because computers require critical thinking, the logical decision would be to prepare students with the critical skills necessary for them to respond accordingly. However, the largest issue in this thinking is that all students would be eligible and prepared for entrance to college. This shift did not include those groups of people who might not have the necessary acumen or desire for success in this new environment.

This situation can be compared to similar events during the Great Depression. That transition, born of a world war and a population moving from an agrarian society to a more industrial, factory-oriented society, took almost seven years. Additionally, it was well understood that the training for particular positions was to be conducted in the workplace. There was no anticipation of students being completely prepared for their position prior to getting the job. College was not a prerequisite. Hiring was based on the ability of a person to learn a new trade and their capacity for maintaining that learning in a speedy and productive way.

Somewhere along the line, capitalism in America has shredded and eliminated job training and put it solely on the shoulders of educational institutions. This requires educational institutions to prepare students for any possible job they might have—even ones that have not yet been created. The conclusion being that if the student is not successful in society, then the institution of education has failed.

The impact of technology upon civilization marks one of the most influential changes since the invention of the wheel or the printing press. The power of information retrieval by any citizen has made the understanding of truth something new for each person. The internet and collective information systems have sped up the process of analysis, along with the monumental ability to capture all the libraries of the world into a tiny phone. Films of the 1950s and '60s depicted vast seas of "secretaries" whose job was to memorialize and organize everything the "thinkers" were creating. From memorandums to setting up travel itineraries, these people have been replaced by technology that anyone can use while walking down the street. SIRI or ALEXA is the new secretary, and she only costs $500! No wonder we have seen a sharp increase in unemployment within the workplace and a gradual shift to a service-based economy. These vital resources are lost to innovation; it's like using your children as remote controls to change the channel on the television set. (Note that this last analogy will only appeal to Generation X and earlier.)

The term "expert" no longer applies to anyone who measures knowledge as expertise, because everyone has the tools in their own pockets to find information. With a cell phone or I-pad, anyone can cross check data from multiple sources at the blink of an eye and form their own "expert" opinions. The effect on American society has been a shift from a knowledge-based society to an interpretation society. Whoever can augment the data to support their particular perspective is a new powerbroker. The fact that the data is completely wrong or not cogent is secondary to the purpose of broadcasting the new result as quickly and often as possible.

If anything from the last ten years has taught educators, it is that the trust in facts has diminished. The ability of people to cross reference and evaluate credibility has been tossed to the side because, by the time you are finished with the credibility process, the news cycle has accepted the previous as truth (or lie) and moved to the next fifty assertions. Knowledge is solely based on the tracking of the current eight-hour cycle of information. Any person who references something in the immediate past is characterized as having created a "gotcha" moment with a personal vendetta attachment or they need to "look at the facts." That is how radiologists—rather than epidemiologists—have become leaders during a major pandemic, and hotel managers are handling intense negotiations with hostile countries.

Education has been unable to prevent this situation from occurring because the models on which it was based are too archaic. The institutional educational system used today was created decades ago to produce factory workers. The mindset was to give kids the tools to survive in society and join the middle class (at a minimum) and our country would then thrive. The problem today is that those jobs don't exist as much anymore. The education for the '60s generation needed to know fractions, angles, and reading in order to successfully construct the world of tomorrow. They didn't need to know elements of power transference, physics, and chemistry to plumb a house. Nor did they need to troubleshoot software and wireless internet issues on a jobsite.

High school education has become stagnant in its contribution to today's society, which has created a large gap between the skillsets of the graduating student and the needs of the workplace.

Schools have made strides to combat this situation but to little advantage. Politicians have turned to educators and given them a mandate to educate America's future leaders. Yet, when educators asked what exactly were the skills needed for that future, they were met with, "I don't know." The Department of Education has worked out the necessary components and processes by incorporating the best procedures from the world—common core. The problem is that Americans do not like change. "I can't even do my third grader's homework" is heard throughout the world as a cry against this process. Interestingly, my grandparents didn't learn algebra or chemistry. They learned baking and woodworking, so they couldn't help me either. This is not to say that elements of chemistry and algebra do not exist within baking and construction. They do. The premise is that the amount and universality of the educational concept have changed. If educators are to create the future of America, they cannot use the same methods used in the past.

There needs to be a return to an apprenticeship style of job training. It could be funded by the corporations, as they wish to have their businesses thrive. It is their responsibility to maintain high levels of educational acumen and to improve their employees' skills. The high school's role is to provide the basic skillsets necessary for living in our society. The 9th –12th-grade high school institutions must return to their prime directive of educating an informed citizenry at a more basic level and not encompass all learned aspects of the workforce.

Teacher Preparation

K-12 credential programs for educators provide the overview necessary for a teacher to walk into a room and start teaching. Most seasoned teachers, however, will state that this education does not completely prepare them for the true experience of being in charge. The strides that have been established to ease new teachers into the classroom have been effective, but the amount of time this program takes before the aspirational teacher can start their career hinders the number of people willing to sacrifice more to commit to this career. The societal expectation for college graduates is that their investments into the education of the student will yield a better job. This has been part of the American dream for generations. Parents and families make large sacrifices to support their college student through the educational journey. Most students lack the capital necessary to complete their studies, so they accumulate large amounts of the debt, hoping that their future income will be sufficient to pay off the debt and its accumulated interest. The credential program structure limits their potential because these graduates, who have invested so much, are asked to take on even more sacrifices. Unfortunately, most potential teachers are forced to choose a different path because they cannot afford to become teachers.

Augmenting the credentialing process with an apprentice program can provide an influx of income for new teachers. The systematic structure of teaching positions, outlined later in this book, allows for each student teacher to master areas of their professional inefficiencies while contributing the newest research, strategies, and perspectives to the team. This new structure allows recent graduates to enter the profession and earn an income at a decent rate while apprenticing—for lack of a better term—in the profession. The new teachers will positively contribute to learning in safer methods while honing their teaching craft with fellow teachers in a collaborative environment. Frequency of formative evaluations will be faster than before in ways that guide these new teachers toward improvement through research, implementation, feedback, and reflection. This inclusion process will allow new graduates to enter the profession and earn a living rather than wait and hope they survive the crucible of another year—or in some cases two years—of college.

Chapter 3

Educational Climate

Today's educational climate is in a state of flux, with multiple changes and societal needs that the world economy and globalization have provided for American society. Since the inception of No Child Left Behind (NCLB), education has focused much of its attention on the process necessary to increase the skills of students to better equip them for the 21st century. The *Turning Points 2000* report provided additional analysis describing the areas that educational institutions need to focus on for students to succeed (Jackson & Davis, 2000). Since then, Common Core State Standards (CCSS) and Race to the Top, provided by the Obama Administration, have continued this legacy.

Concentration on skills-oriented teaching methods must continue so the American student can compete in a global economy. Goldman and Pellegrino (2015) concluded that the current educational system falls short of filling all the needs of its students for the 21st century. According to these researchers, the most crucial elements are the perspectives of how people learn and the styles of assessment (Goldman & Pellegrino, 2015). These conclusions echoed the previous findings of Hattie's (2012) meta-analysis, which stated that the most influential element of student learning is the teacher's view of their role and the constant evaluation of impacts on student learning.

Blueprint for Reform provided a structure and plan for schools throughout the United States to improve the process of education across all areas (U.S. Department of Education, 2010). Within that framework is a directive for all schools to increase teacher knowledge in order to effectively intervene with students. Gulbranson (2016) summarized Strouse (2001), who contended that education should help prepare children by giving them the social tools necessary to survive in society. The future of American education will evolve from the concerted efforts of teachers to progress in the art of teaching rather than continuing to treat it as a science (Hattie, 2012).

COVID-19 has forced every educator to reflect on each aspect of their teaching craft because of their separation from students. The separation from the student has required new methods of engagement never before thought of . In the traditional classroom setting, the teacher would be able to adjust the speed, depth, or clarity of instruction by the physical responses of students, based on immediate feedback from the students' behaviors. The limitations of response and attention by students has caused teachers to solely rely on personal reflection and survey-style data to engage students. Teachers are forced to use data as their measure of success because that is the sole form of feedback they are getting from students.

Finally, the teacher is addressing the monumental task of engaging students when *they*—the students—have the time or ability to do so. The necessity of bending education around the environment of the student has been a wakeup call for some educators.

Student access to the internet is inconsistent at times, which limits their ability to be in class. Internet crashes are commonplace because the entire family is online at the same time. Student responses are not occurring, not because they are being defiant but because their sisters or brothers are having a meltdown in the same room. Classes are being interrupted by a barking dog—it may even be the teacher's dog—because someone is not muted. The learning environment has needed to become a more flexible entity than the rows of chairs in the "teacher's" room where the teacher is the master of the domain. Families are reprioritizing the education of their children right now, and some are willing to sacrifice it for the shorter-term strategies of survival. If the choice is the internet bill or food for the month, education will not be the first choice.

The conversation of access for students has become a reality in many districts. The gap in education caused by the inequitable use of the internet is more apparent than ever. Districts and municipalities have addressed this issue in the past, which is similar to the disparities of the Jim Crowe laws and their "separate-but-equal" policies. The concept is that if the student has access to the raw material—the book—they will be able to thrive. This has allowed the district to relinquish responsibility of the student's achievement because the "opportunity" was offered.

The pandemic has highlighted the issue that person-to-person intervention shrinks the education gap more than just access to raw material. Students need terms and procedures clarified. Methodically stepped instructions to difficult concepts need to be available to all students, with continual checking of understanding throughout the process. The challenge is to maximize the information age for *all* students, with these needs in mind.

Inherent within the new challenges the pandemic has raised in our society is the resiliency of the student. Lonora Chu shines some light on the problems with Western education in her book *Little Soldiers* (2017). In the book, she describes the need for parents to see teachers as experts and support student learning from home. If the teacher states that the student is not measuring up in a skill, the parent must find the resources and time for practice so the student can master the standard. Chu goes on to outline that a key difference between Eastern and Western education is the Western attitude that learning is tied to an ability. If a student doesn't like the subject, it must be because of an inability to master that subject, which creates a world of excuses and adjustments from everyone but the child. Eastern schools view education with the premise that *all* students can learn things through hard work. A student's low performance is seen through the lens of shame, which causes the family to respond with whatever is needed for the student to succeed. Also, motivation is not controlled by the student but by the environment. The consequences of a student not working hard enough are felt at school and at home. These measures trigger negative motivation through shame. This view can be harsh for students and does affect their self-esteem. However, the school is not responsible for the child's self-esteem; that is the family's role.

The concepts of shame, grit, and perseverance in Western education have been reclassified through feelings and not results. There is not a single lesson that a person has learned that changed their life profoundly without pain or strife. Pain can be productive as long as it does not break the student. Unfortunately, the current system has chosen to eliminate pain at all times in order to motivate students to perform. There needs to be a change in the American mindset that will encourage students to be self-motivated while trusting the educational process. They must comprehend the possible quality of their product and be willing to honestly accept the results. Lastly, students must break through initial obstacles for a greater purpose—understanding that struggle is a part of learning.

Chapter 4

Current Methods

E ducation has evolved throughout the ages to provide the best possible education for children. As the number of teachers increased with the adoption of the Industrial Revolution model, the most effective method of improving education has been to bring teachers together in order to find the best possible methods. A summary of the most proven methods is provided in this chapter.

Collaboration

The need for collaboration within schools was generated from the understanding that the school is responsible for the whole child. Collaboration provides consistencies in instruction, which, in turn, creates inclusion among stakeholders. A school district can better guarantee a level of instruction for each child's education when it has created a collaborative structure for the success of instruction (Taylor, 2013). The transactional change of bringing teachers together to share the happenings within their lessons is meant to gain insight on dealing with student behavior and aligning their instruction across the subject or grade for consistency of learning throughout the school site (Little, 2003; Szczesiul & Huizenga, 2015). The premise was to increase instructional practice through the sharing of experiences and struggles among teachers while forming new ideas for success.

Mitchell, Ripley, Adams, and Raju (2011) hypothesized a direct correlation between levels of trust and collaboration. They asserted that collaboration requires "parties to come together and to share both responsibility and accountability" (Mitchell et al., 2011, p. 147). Furthermore, effective collaboration needs members to "trust the other party will act in a manner that can be counted on and that is in the best interest of all concerned" (Mitchell et al., 2011, p. 147). They described the benefits of collaboration on the different aspects of the school site and came to the conclusion that collaboration ultimately benefits the capacity of the teacher, which in turn builds on the school's ability to change (Mitchell et al., 2011).

The desired benefits of collaboration come in many different forms. Taylor (2013) identified four categories of benefit from common planning time (CPT):

(a) CPT built a sense of community and mutual support

(b) teachers with CPT generated new knowledge and effectiveness

(c) teachers with CPT were committed to support students' social, emotional, and intellectual development

(d) CPT benefited the whole school, not just the team (p. 118)

Discussions that center on instruction guarantee that student learning across the entire school site is the same in content and assessment (Szczesiul & Huizenga, 2015). Student intervention ideas between collaborating teachers are generated to engage students in the classroom and deal with behavioral challenges. Instructionally, the school site becomes a more unified program of education that is easier to understand.

Ancillary benefits have occurred from the implementation of collaboration on school sites. Higher levels of relationships within the school teams have been generated. Teacher bonding with the school site becomes stronger (Taylor, 2013). New research and strategies are shared among the group for consideration, which fosters further sharing among the participants (Adams, 2009). Methodologies, like grading and teaching style, are debated, with general consensus reached by most parties for increased fidelity of instruction. Most of all, teachers began sharing methods that challenged them, and they sought advice on how to overcome those challenges (Mertens, Anfara, Caskey, & Flowers, 2013). This shared learning journey generates higher levels of pedagogy and intervention.

Little (2003) studied the concept of sharing among teachers outside of the classroom. Her findings described the daily accomplishments for the teacher within the collaborative climate. She suggested that the occurrences within a separate collaborative meeting are the following:

> The groups demonstrably reserve time to identify and examine problems of practice; they elaborate those problems in ways that open up new considerations and possibilities; they readily disclose their uncertainties and dilemmas and invite comment and advice from others; and artifacts of classroom practice (student work, lesson plans, and the like) are made accessible. In all these ways, the groups display dispositions, norms, and habits conducive to teacher learning and the improvement of teaching practice (p. 938).

These additional avenues of inquiry and decision making simultaneously enhance the craft of teaching in multidirectional manners with numerous pedagogical strategies. Therefore, it is not a surprise for leaders to see different methods to control or organize such a dynamic phenomenon.

Collaboration positively affects the efficiency of teachers. Gyesaw (2012) noticed a teacher's struggle of wanting to be a part of a collegial group while maintaining self-importance. Teachers are more productive in the community format while advancing their teaching methods (Corcoran & Silander, 2009; Doğan & Yurtseven, 2018). Teacher inductions become a teacher-led endeavor rather than administrative (Allen, 2013; Tschannen-Moran, 2001). However, Gyesaw's (2012) conclusions do not support the high level of "joint work" described by Little (2003). The idea that a minority of teachers have intense work yet all must produce demonstrates that teachers must come together through support, thereby building confidence for future work. When teachers are empowered, they are more likely to produce better quality instruction (Avolio et al., 2004).

Professional Learning Communities

DuFour et al. (2010) are the founders of the concept of a professional learning community (PLC), and their continued research improves this process. Many others have investigated the different elements of the PLC process and expanded them for success. From ethnic and special education implications to adaptation to CCSS and Smarter Balanced Assessment Consortium (SBAC) testing processes, many broad challenges currently face teachers. Research shows that PLC groups must bond together for sharing to occur on a regular basis (Bretz, 2013; Harvey & Drolet, 2004). There must be a high level of what Amy Edmondson (1999) identifies as psychological safety for all members in order for them to truly share all facets of their teaching strategies. Caine and Caine's (2010) analysis reinforced this idea in recognizing that "participants in a good learning community find that it helps to have colleagues with whom to talk things through, reflect, analyze, and discuss" (p. 17). The basic and continual communication about student progress is the element that provides the program's success.

PLCs have become the standard approach by districts for student achievement (Smith, 2015). The processes within the PLC meeting allow teachers to systematically improve instruction for all students within any district (DuFour et al., 2010). Efforts from these teacher teams positively affect student outcomes when the teams work collaboratively toward improved instruction (Bretz, 2013). Hord (2004) described the five different dimensions that exist in a PLC as:

◊   Supportive and shared leadership
◊   Shared values and vision
◊   Collective learning and application of learning
◊   Supportive conditions
◊   Cheer practice (p. 7)

Central to the PLC process is the need for teachers to work effectively as a unit. With successful teamwork, PLC departments will raise scores and learning for students at their site (Gulbransen, 2016; Polhemus, 2010).

Leaders of PLC groups must influence all characteristics of team effectiveness in order for the teachers to generate any outcome (Harvey & Drolet, 2004). The groups journey through the creation of "teamness," as articulated by Jones and Bearley (2001), to forge a cohesive unit. A significant characteristic of the team is the ability of its members to maintain high levels of interaction for successful decisions and implementation of ideas (Harvey & Drolet, 2004).

The core of member interaction is the feeling that each member can take risks without ridicule, or what Edmondson (1999) defined as psychological safety.

Teacher sharing and collaboration is central to the success of the PLC (Bretz, 2013; Dever & Lash, 2013; Hadar & Brody, 2010). A requirement for this collaboration is the ability for all members to openly share with their colleagues, which Bloom and Vitcov (2010) described as an opportunity to build deeper trusting relationships. Unfortunately, the research does not describe applicable methods for fostering this sharing. Hadar and Brody (2010) articulated that there should be a "safe and comfortable environment for the talk about mistakes and attempting new teaching methods" (p. 1646). It is presumed that teachers will openly share their mistakes and seek better practices based on their professionalism.

Purpose

The premise behind DuFour et al.'s (2010) idea of the PLC is that, through examination of data and shared knowledge, each teacher will advance his or her own craft of teaching. By measuring and analyzing the success of the classroom, teachers will be motivated to better their instruction, thereby advancing student achievement (Little, 2003). This position relies on a few assumptions. One assumption is that teachers are knowledgeable enough about the practice of teaching that they will solve any problems that might arise (Andrews, 2014; Dalal, 2013). Next, designated groups will work homogeneously toward common goals (DuFour & Eaker, 1998; Polhemus, 2010). Finally, teachers must willingly participate in the processes outlined in the PLC meetings and consistently follow through with their commitments.

Hord (2004) outlined the dimensions of collaborative PLCs: "(1) supportive and shared leadership, (2) shared values and vision, (3) collective learning and application of learning (formerly identified as collective creativity), (4) supportive conditions, and (5) shared personal practice" (p. 7). All of these elements rely on the team collaborating together in each aspect for success. Cohesion of the group is what ensures the effectiveness of the work (Harvey & Drolet, 2004). The absence of any one of these elements is a hindrance to the productivity of the team.

Team Dynamics

According to DuFour et al. (2010), the PLC environment is supposed to be one of collegial learning. Assessment creation by the team commits the group to common elements of the curriculum, which increases fidelity at the school site. Data analysis identifies areas of need, along with successful strategies for students. Proven pedagogy based on school population is shared for implementation comparison. Troubled teachers openly share frustrations and mistakes with their colleagues in order to gain insight from peers in the hopes of advancing their practice. Conflict that surrounds important issues and decisions is resolved in positive ways (Lencioni, 2012). New methods and initiatives are presented for adoption to ensure cohesion among all members. In sum, all aspects of teaching are evaluated, shared, and improved so that teachers learn the best practices for their students at that time.

The influence of personality on the team affects the creativity produced. Gong, Cheung, Wang, and Huang's (2012) integrative model shows that proactive personalities foster information exchanges, which generate trust and create ideas among the group. They found that this perspective advances a new dimension of psychological safety with "the finding that the workplace trust relationship relates positively to individual creativity [and] supports the psychological safety perspective at the individual level" (Gong et al., 2012, p. 1628). There is benefit for team members who possess the internal drive to better themselves and seek out methods to create that improvement. However, the challenge for some members is the courage to proactively risk themselves rather than react to negative responses.

Leadership

Leadership in PLCs was meant to be solely based on the teachers motivating themselves (Gyesaw, 2012). The concept of self-driven meetings was proposed to allow a high level of trust and sharing, thus creating an environment of learning among teachers (DuFour et al., 2010; Senge et al., 2012). Administrators are to assume a more transformational role for the success of the PLC by fostering an environment in which to amplify the team's talents (Eaker, DuFour, & Burnette, 2002; Moller, 2006). Avolio et al. (2004) referenced Shamir et al. (1998), who postulated that transformational leaders sway commitment by affecting members' intrinsic value to the organization. Administrators ensure that the workings of the PLC align with district goals and culture of the school site (Avolio et al., 2004). New resources for the team are provided by the administrator to ensure the process runs efficiently; i.e., data results, testing platforms, and curriculum. The administrative role is to support the PLC leader's needs of keeping the team accountable to the processes and to their fellow team members. The true leader of the PLC is the teacher leader, not the administrator.

Currently, implementation of the PLC process has been conducted in a Draconian manner with the administrator having direct oversight of the meeting (Moller, 2006). The chilling effect this produces on sharing and collaboration is monumental and is a true disservice to the school and the teaching profession. The true leader within the PLC is one who facilitates the dynamics within the team while fulfilling the expectations of the group.

Hargreaves and Fink (2006) outlined eight strengths that good leaders possess:

◊ Modeling and building strong and rewarding relationships by paying attention to the human side of school change

◊ Establishing a high trust environment

◊ Developing and renewing a culture of learning and improvement at all levels through problem solving, inquiry, and intelligent, evidence-informed decision making

◊ Helping the school community to develop and commit to a cohesive and compelling purpose that prevents dissipation of initiative and effort

◊ Stimulating a culture of professional entrepreneurship in innovations and ideas that benefit student learning

◊ Establishing and regulating grown-up, professional norms of civil argument and productive debate

◊ Ensuring the voices of minority members of the culture always receive a proper hearing

◊ Doing all this within an unswerving commitment to improving all students' learning and achievement, especially for those who are furthest behind. (p. 560)

These attributes to great leadership require in-depth interactions with the team on a regular basis, with the absence of evaluative pressures with leadership distributed throughout the school site (DuFour et al., 2010; Hargreaves & Fink, 2006).

Avolio et al. (2004) examined the interrelationship between transformational leadership and organizational commitment. They concluded that there is a correlation between the feelings of people being empowered by their leaders and their ability to make crucial decisions. The result is larger commitment by the employee to the company and a genuine concern for others' wellbeing. Employees also experienced increased productivity and work quality based on these feelings (Avolio et al., 2004). One factor the researchers detail as influential is the physical distance between leaders and employees (Avolio et al., 2004). Administrators are removed from the inner workings of the PLC on a continual basis. The result is that the distance interferes with the empowerment necessary for the PLC to work at optimal levels. The best solution is to shift the leadership role to the department chairs within the environment.

Professional Learning Communities (PLC)

Struggles with the PLC model come from lack of commitment, which is manifested in complete refusal or reluctant participation with extreme limitations. Teachers become passive in the process and lose the true focus of the program (Muñoz & Branham, 2016). Some teachers refuse to participate in the process because they believe the student is solely to blame for the assessment numbers, and they refuse to reflect on their own methods of instruction (Horn et al., 2017). Some departments are not clear about the purpose and process of PLCs, which alters the way they function, with troubling results (Joyce, 2004; Little, 2003). These obstacles stifle every level of the process and collapse any hope of improved teaching.

PLC teams are effective with high levels of trust (Hord, 2004). Teachers who do not trust department leadership will hold back on sharing. School leadership that does not create a positive culture in PLCs fosters apprehension or denial (Peters, 2013). Miscommunication or perceived attacks on the teacher suppress enthusiasm in the process (Tschannen-Moran, 2014). Additionally, high levels of support and encouragement through difficult work within the PLC must be cultivated in order to prevent gradual apprehension (Eaker et al., 2002).

Trust

Mitchell et al. (2011) explored the definition of trust and argued that there must be an element of risk in order for trust to be established. According to Lencioni (2012), trust is the foundation for teams to become cohesive units. Trust is vital to work within the school site (Mitchell et al., 2011; Tschannen-Moran & Hoy, 1998). Mitchell et al. (2011) concluded, "When teachers trust the principal, their colleagues, and parents, they are more likely to collaborate with their fellow colleagues on instructional decisions" (p. 164). Cranston (2011) found that high levels of relational trust led to more effective collaboration. Peters (2013) found the inverse: established collaboration creates trusting relationships through vulnerability. The reciprocal nature of these relationships continually increases the levels of information, sharing, and productivity.

Relational trust is established from intrapersonal, interpersonal, and organizational levels (Bryk & Schneider, 2002). As information is shared among participants, it causes a dynamic environment where the support and strains of the work affect the relationship.

The relationship currency exchanged during these times makes all parties evaluate their social capital with others (Penuel, Fishman, Yamaguchi, & Gallagher, 2007; Penuel, Frank, & Krause, 2006).

The central elements needed to establish trust among people is the sharing of oneself in authentic honesty and the proven commitments between those same individuals (Tschannen-Moran, 2014). This evolving relationship begins at the first introduction and continues with every following interaction (Tschannen-Moran, 2014). Tschannen-Moran (2014) described a trustworthy individual as a person who needs to "demonstrate benevolence, reliability, competence, honesty and openness" (p. 314). Weisman (2010) and Escalante (2019) reinforced these characteristics through the Values Institute's five domains of competence, consistency, concern, candor, and connection.

The exploration of mistrust has focused on the methods of resolving conflicts in a productive way in order to maintain high levels of performance. Trust is a fragile thing to maintain, given the dynamic elements of individuals and their environments. In most teams, the opportunities for mistrust are greater because people are assigned to a group in which they cannot choose their teammates. According to Bies and Tripp (1996), trust is violated by damaging the person's identity or the norms of the group. Trust violations also hinder organizational performance (Tschannen-Moran, 2001). Wicks, Berman, and Jones (1999) stated that dealing with mistrust in an optimal situation occurs with the violation happening within a range of the relationship's current position, thereby allowing the violator to regain enough trust to maintain the same relative level when the conflict is completed.

Psychological Safety

The sharing of instructional strategies with one another via appropriately received feedback can increase the skill of the teacher and can advance his or her learning and instruction (Kimmons, 2016). Research conducted examining the interactions of people within a PLC is limited (Cranston, 2011; Little, 2003). The application of the new feedback allows the team to shift the mindset of the group to a clinical exploration rather than a job. Horn et al. (2017) described this phenomenon as the mindset struggle of being a *doer* rather than a *thinker*. By exploring different styles and strategies within lessons, the PLC exhibits conversational learning to advance the teaching craft.

Edmondson's (1999) seminal study of team effectiveness established the term *psychological safety* by her work with hospitals. She examined the levels at which nurses were willing to admit mistakes to their colleagues and superiors within all facets of their work. As Edmonson stated, "An aim of the present study was to investigate whether beliefs about the interpersonal context vary between teams in the same organization, as well as to examine their effects on team outcomes" (p. 352). From this initial work, the focus of effective team interaction has continued to grow in a variety of areas. Project Aristotle, sponsored by Google (2012), reinforced the need for high levels of psychological safety among teams in a corporate setting for optimal effectiveness. Throughout the research, led by Edmondson's (2018) work, it was established that psychological safety is not a personality trait or a chemistry dynamic within the team, but an environmental situation that can be influenced. All findings found trepidation on the part of workers to share with their bosses (Edmondson, 2018). Organizations must establish a psychologically safe environment in order to combat the conditions that hinder progress, or as Edmondson identified, as VUCA conditions: volatility, uncertainty, complexity, and ambiguity. Edmondson established a correlation between levels of psychological safety and job performance, which is expressed with the following graphic in Figure 1:

Figure 1. How Psychological Safety Relates to Performance Standards

	Low Standards	High Standards
High Psychological Safety	*Comfort Zone*	*Learning & High Performance Zone*
Low Psychological Safety	*Apathy Zone*	*Anxiety Zone*

Adapted from *The Fearless Organization: Creating Psychological Safety in the Workplace For Learning, Innovation, and Growth,* by A. Edmondson, 2018, p. 18. Hoboken, NJ: John Wiley & Sons.

Ultimately, according to Edmondson in a 2019 podcast, a psychologically safe environment is one where "people believe they can bring their full self to work and more specifically it means they feel they can speak up and their ideas will be welcomed" (Crowley, 2019). A psychological study has found that psychological safety builds positive relationships between team members, strengthens relationship ties, and increases advice sharing among team members (Schulte, Cohen, & Klein, 2012). Lencioni (2012) corroborated this idea, stating that when "colleagues are truly committed to something, they confront one another about issues without feeling defensiveness or backlash" (p. 55). It is a necessity that psychological safety be established within small teams for the optimal productivity of the organization.

Use of psychological safety in the educational environment is being explored as a component of a larger relationship dynamic. Psychological safety has been confirmed as a large contributor to trust (Bloom & Vitcov, 2010). Hutt (2007) studied experiential learning spaces in dealing with the high anxiety subject of math and detailed the need for more examination of psychological safety among teachers. The term *experiential learning space* derives from the Kolb framework of concrete experience, reflective observation, abstract conceptualization, and active experimentation (Kolb & Kolb, 2017). However, the Kolb framework is not a source of psychological safety but the result of establishing safety within the individual. Hutt (2007) agreed with previous research that psychological safety occurs within "a well-bounded experiential learning space as a norm and shared cultural belief" (p. 77).

Choo et al. (2004) found that learning from sharing within a psychologically safe environment is different from more structured methods. This corroborates the findings that team psychological safety has a positive relationship to team learning (Raes et al., 2013). Psychological safety also needs to be established in order to change teacher practices and increase productivity within the classroom (Wagner et al., 2006). Instructional practices are enhanced and innovated within teams that have high levels of psychological safety. The need to build the capacity of teacher teams to create the highest levels of psychological safety will be paramount for the added success of teachers and students.

Section 2

The Annihilation of Education

"The structures were never able to withstand the monster that was 50 times the size of the structure"

Chapter 5

Learning Lessons from COVID-19

The COVID-19 pandemic has highlighted weaknesses in the educational system more than at any other time in history. For decades the educational system was directed in a broad way to make society better only within the traditional frameworks that had been established since the industrialization age. Forcing students to remain at home because of a deadly virus that can be spread just by being in the same room has caused educators to question every aspect of their teaching methods. Some educators and institutions have played the waiting game. They have put their heads in the sand and ignored the situation for a long time, but the COVID-19 pandemic has truly brought that to the forefront. Every day they manage the situation at hand with the hope that "this will pass" and everything will go back to "normal." The mistake in using this method is the belief that the previous system was completely successful. The hard lesson for some educators is the realization that their needs and interests within the class are sometimes superseded by the students' needs of survival.

Other educators have used this opportunity to finetune their craft to a semi-new norm. They integrate their lessons into digital processes. They learn the different technological meeting spaces. They explore new learning platforms they have previously ignored. The benefit of this particular situation is that the teachers— Mohammed (2017) calls them "resistors"—have been forced to integrate the advancement of technology that their districts have been advocating for the last decade. The current situation has made some teachers' effectiveness blatantly obvious to all. So these teachers finally made the effort to implement technology because their teaching reputations were finally at stake. For other teachers, this horrific time has been seized as an opportunity to reimagine what they see as education.

Truly balancing grace and understanding with the needs of educating the next generation has some teachers assessing their influence within a larger society. Not taking advantage of this time to re-innovate and rethink how teaching and the craft of learning are done is detrimental to society in general. This situation might not be the only one. There could be other pandemics in the future.

Societal strife and new styles of warfare could limit the accessibility of students to actually go to school for fear of their lives. Similar to the great generations of the 1930s and '40s, education must be flexible once again for families and societies who are just trying to stay alive. It must be flexible enough for long absences so students can assist with the needs of their families. The educational system must be flexible enough to support new initiatives similar to the New Deal implemented by President Roosevelt in the 1930s. The educational school year was originally created to support the farming/harvest season, so why can that not be taken advantage of or recognized in its full potential today?

For far too long, the soundbites of politicians have influenced education and its goals to support students throughout the United States. These guidelines and visions are not negative things that educators ignore but should be embraced to better the next generation. For the longest time, the motto has been "students should be able to go to college." That is not a bad goal. However, a gap was created when society focused on the wrong word. Society for too long has focused on the word "should" and given all of its efforts to guide—and in some cases force—students into an area they are either not prepared for or do not even want. Essential elements of this new process of education are a shift to the word "able." Every student, regardless of societal position, should have the *opportunity* to excel and to strive for greatness in the United States, especially in the educational arena. Education should continue to evolve through the measurement of student abilities and the ability of the educational system to meet those abilities.

It is in this spirit that we have the opportunity to change and truly innovate the learning experience for the betterment of all post-pandemic students. New opportunities can be seized and created for society to benefit student access to learning and a re-prioritizing of educational importance. Creating a system that can continue to educate students and keep society moving forward, regardless of locality, needs to be of the highest importance in the immediate future.

Section 3

The Call to Change

One key thing I noticed was that when the one child would destroy the castles, the others would express their disappointment and then immediately start the game over again.

The standard question that surfaces is why change the system? The system seems to have worked for the last century, and there have been strides in improving the education experience of most students. Milestones have been made in serving those students with learning disabilities. Pathways have been created for students who are new to the United States to acquire a performing level of English. Curriculums have been aligned to standards so that all states have similar expectations of high school graduates. College and career pathways have been streamlined with clear goals. School district accountability measures have been augmented to reflect a more comprehensive measuring system.

So the true answer as to whether the school system needs to change is that it ultimately doesn't. Society could reestablish the same processes it has always had and continue to progress at a glacial pace. It could continue to entitle students and not prepare them with the skills needed for their future careers. They could continue to produce students who have an extremely limited knowledge of how the country's government works and their role in the process. Schools can continue to offer educational experiences for the interests of teachers instead of the students, with a miniscule amount of accountability. Lastly, the world could continue doing the same thing it has always done and consider COVID-19 as a fluke situation that will probably not happen again in our lifetimes because it was a once-in-a-century event.

OR

The educational community could seize this opportunity to really innovate the way children learn. School could have a new way of existing within everyone's daily life. It could truly reflect its purpose in the world. The school could be flexible to the needs of the students *in* their lives rather than be something that students are to mold their lives *to*. The school could be a place where *learning* is the focus the entire time, and teachers' most valuable talents are utilized.

Section 4

Examining Each Block

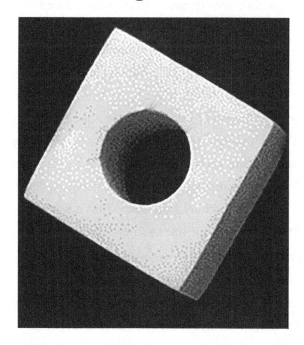

They would look at the blocks and evaluate their strengths and weaknesses. Sometimes, they would ask to redesign the current block with statements like, "Is there a block with a round, flat and round?"

Chapter 6

Redefining the Role of School in Society

In creating a new tomorrow for education, the image of school needs to be reimagined. Education's contribution to society needs to be evaluated and a redefinition of the educational institution's role within society needs to be rearticulated. For too long the school has been the place where all problems are handled. Hunger, mental health, suicide prevention, behavioral changes, and law enforcement have been made the responsibility of the schools. Whenever a societal problem rears its head on the daily news, leaders turn to educators to solve it for the sake of the future.

Leaders must evaluate the entire school experience for students and the contribution each component serves for the future of that student. In a more simplistic way, society needs to figure out what it actually needs from schools and then what it wants from schools. Our society can then prioritize the needs over the wants and allocate the appropriate resources to the needs.

The school of tomorrow is not a place where students will sit for long hours, being fed information, as described by Freire (2018). This philosophy describes a world where knowledge is deposited into student minds so society can withdraw the benefit. Teachers are the "sages" that indoctrinate societal knowledge and all other exploration is shunned. It is time that the banking model is turned on its head. Schools need to become a resource place of self-investigation for students. Yes, schools have the obligation to provide what is known as an informed citizenry, as outlined by Thomas Jefferson. They must be able to prepare the students of tomorrow with the ability to read, explore their world through science, and calculate different aspects of our world through math. Technology can be maximized to effectively guide students for self-education.

Technology has drastically improved education for students; that is an undeniable fact. What is under dispute is the effectiveness of teachers to leverage technology in the educational environment for its maximal use in informing students. Since the beginning of the Information Age, a premise has emerged that students must learn how to use technology *from teachers* in order for it to be effective. The problem with this paradigm is that the student often knows more about the technology and its effectiveness than the person teaching them. This situation is similar to a horse trainer teaching young people how to drive a car. There are similarities in how to steer and how to adjust speed, but there are so many differences as to how the technology works that makes the education of the horse trainer completely obsolete. When educators can realize that students have the ability for self-exploration, then the true paradigm of education can make a shift.

College has always been referred as the place where people "find themselves" and declare what they want to do with their lives. By adopting a form of that model within the high school process, students will be more focused and more motivated to achieve higher levels of education, hence achieving higher measurements of success in their future careers. The high school diploma will no longer be a gateway to adulthood but a measurement of effectiveness in students' contribution to society. The stigma of exclusion for some who don't gain a high school diploma will be diminished because these people will make other contributions to society.

The "Greatest Generation" (Brokaw 2004) of the 1930s and post-World War II did not create a stigma for people who walked off the battlefield after great examples of valor and then drove a truck for 40 years. There was pride in work because of the experiences. The problem is the fact that the communal society of America does not recognize the different stripes of individuals within its society.

World War II was a global effort with a common enemy, so it was easy for every American to respect that these people fought against what was termed as evil. Very few people blamed veterans who came back from the war and struggled with alcoholism and dealing with their reestablishment into society. So life in a battlefield was just another day at the office. What changed was the recognition of society to the strife those veterans endured. The situation might have been more gruesome but dealing with death was the same. In the end, when those young GIs walked off the train to reenter society, society recognized them as men and not weekend people from a certain area or neighborhood. That is not to say there wasn't discrimination, both in gender and race, after World War II. However, what did change was the ability for people to see the absurdity of the discrimination because of the common strife that was known by all Americans.

How can today's educational society come to the same respect for individuals choosing their own paths? Some current students are forced into situations where they have to exhibit complete valor and bravery or face death every day. When dealing with current situations of societal poverty, domestic abuse, neighborhood violence, discrimination, or other forms of societal strife, these victims are blamed. These individuals see it—and experience it—but no one pays attention, except for those in the classrooms. Students have essentially become veterans of the educational battlefield, which is why some families would prefer to not have students in school at all. It is up to the educators of the world to create an environment flexible enough that kids can come in and out of the educational structure based on societal and environmental factors. However, all avenues connecting those educational environments should be outlined in order for the student to be successful.

The GI Bill was a major success for all of America because all veterans, from famous men like Bob Dole to relatively anonymous ones like Nick Cloo (my grandfather), had the opportunity to gain the training they desired to better their family's lives. Without the GI Bill, a number of senators and leaders of our country would never have attained their levels of success. The professors, the thinkers, the CEOs, and the advocates would have never achieved their titles without these humble ancestors taking advantage of these opportunities. This opportunity for students to be "able" to succeed must be given and structured at the high school level.

In order for students to be successful, the educational society must maximize the talents of every individual teacher. Additionally, the opportunities for growth and learning of teachers must continually be observed, evaluated, and promoted so that teachers can model lifelong learning and investigate the latest methods of education for the betterment of all students. A cohesive instructional strategy needs to be decided upon and adjusted at a moment's notice, given the latest technology that can come from anywhere. Ten years ago, no one would have ever thought students would pick up their own computers from school and run their entire educational lives from their living rooms.

The educational society must continue to evolve and advance this method of process so that students can be ahead of everyone else in the world. The complete learning process must include genuine intervention and true spiral teaching for all students. The opportunities for interventions and supports must be provided, along with extension opportunities for those students who excel in specific areas. If a student is really motivated and completely talented—within the realms of revolutionary history, for example—then the student must be given the space, time, and opportunity to continue that exploration.

Education, along with many of our other processes, needs a bottom-up innovation. It needs to reassess the needs of the future and create a structure that supports the desired outcomes. The first thing people consider before building a structure—house, office building, park facilities, or bathroom—is the proposed goal for the space. California will spend trillions of dollars on an arena that holds 100,000 people for events but won't concentrate the same energy on the six million students who are supposed to be their best investment. Educational institutions must tear down what they know and rebuild a new structure of education that reflects the new historical era, not just give another update.

Spaces, structures, times, and processes need to be reimagined. The purpose and focus of each building need to be reconceptualized, based on what our experiences perceive the demands of the future will be. The procedures and times need to be reevaluated solely based on the necessary outcomes of students. Whether the school day becomes longer, year round, or shorter should depend on society's needs and not the parents' needs. One key conclusion from the latest pandemic is that schools have truly become what was always rumored: glorified babysitting services. This must change.

Before proceeding with the reinvention of education, an honest conversation must be held by the organization as to its sole purpose. To be clear, this is not another exercise in recreating the mission statement. I will frequently ask people of all walks of life, "Why do we have high school?" or "What is the central purpose of high school?" I rarely get an answer, let alone a coherent one. These are the questions that must drive this innovation. These explorations need to be seen through the lens of history and society, and *not* through educators. Some questions to ask should be:

◊   What singular responsibility should society require of high school?

◊   What is high school's contribution to a student's entire life?

◊   What should be the limitations for schools in a student's life?

◊   What should high schools really be responsible for?

The product of this crucial conversation is the prime directive of the organization that the high schools must restructure education around. All aspects of the education must *directly* feed this directive without exception. The school structure must then be refocused to support this directive.

The following chapters outline some innovations that reimagine teaching, along with some considerations when implementing those innovations. Figure 2 provides a graphic understanding of the concept.

Figure 2: Prime Directive Concept Map

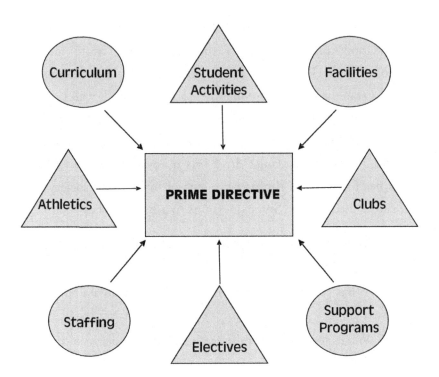

The interesting thing is that schools are not constitutionally bound to generate a certain educational level. There is no language in the United States Constitution that states schools should even exist. The Supreme Court gave this responsibility to the states in 1973 with its verdict on San Antonio Independent School District v. Rodriguez. The Education Commission of the United States reviewed the state constitutions of all 50 states in looking for the language for education (2016). An examination of their review shows that states generally have the following requirements in education:

1. Public education must be free
2. Each state must provide an educational school location
3. The school year must be conducted (The longest outlined time is 9 months in North Carolina.)

The federal government places no other responsibilities for education on the states, which means that additional responsibilities are outlined by each state's governors. These must be clear, long-term directives that schools should strictly adhere to.

A message of caution needs to be given here. Educators are wired to be generous and supportive of their students. They treat these children as if they were their own kids, and that is not wrong. It is this lens that keeps teachers in the K-12 arena for their entire careers. However, the result in leadership is the misconception that teachers know what is best for kids. The consequence is that the current system gives education and activities that students—especially at the high school level—do not *need*. It is nice to provide different, interest-based electives. Clubs that explore different viewpoints of society are interesting. Exploring different applications of these interests is great for the papers. But they are not focused on the sole reason for educating. These discussions need to solely focus on the high school's responsibility to society and history, not the life of a child.

When educational institutions can articulate the true prime directive of a high school, all other aspects of the school must be generated to support this specific purpose. This directive will provide the credibility necessary to reject the whims and ancillary recommendations of other societal entities. There will be aspects of the current school system that will need to change and be directed toward the proper departments. The final result will be a clear pathway for all citizens as to the purpose, structure, and goal of high school.

The Civic Duty of Schools

There has been much conversation regarding the school's position in educating the children of tomorrow. The school institution is finding there is no way to appease most of the population with the education that is currently being given to their children, because America is a melting pot of different ideas, beliefs, and moral perspectives. There is little consensus on most things these days, and government education is one of them. The George W. Bush Administration initiated the No Child Left Behind program with the understanding that all children should have a proficient level of knowledge across the entire country. The educational system spent years supporting that directive. However, they seem to have missed it with regard to civics. In high school, specifically, generations of students have graduated with the most minimal understanding of how government works. Structurally, this occurs because the civics courses are given as a semester course during the students' senior year. The end result is generations of people who do not even know how a piece of legislation is passed. They do not know the difference between the House of Representatives and the Senate. They do not know the roles and responsibilities of the Executive Branch or the Judicial Branch. They do not know the responsibilities of a state government or local government and the effect that any form of government has upon them and their families. It is in this realm that there needs to be a change. The educational institution has a civic duty to ensure that the students who leave their gates possess a basic knowledge of how their representative government is supposed to work.

In order to accomplish this goal, which does align with the prime directive of any school, the course for government must become a year-long course and be given in the sophomore or freshman year of high school. This expanded curriculum needs to incorporate not only the evolution of government and its inner workings, but also the structure and workings of state and local governments. The culminating assessment for this course should be the passage of the United State Citizenship test that is provided for all incoming immigrants. This test should be the direct replacement of the High School Exit Exam and require passage before a diploma is issued. *This* is the basic knowledge that *every* citizen must have to exist within our country, and it is a travesty that the education system is not leading the way in this venture.

It is very understandable that this is a controversial course, which makes it understandable how the educational system has slowly stepped away from this responsibility. Parents continually accuse schools of brainwashing their children with beliefs or political perspectives that are different from their own. They proclaim that schools should not try to persuade their children to think differently than the family and should stay out of their business. These arguments are not unfounded and should be taken into consideration when creating the curriculum for this course. Again, this course would be the inner workings and responsibilities of all dimensions of federal, state, and local governments. It would define each purpose and resource so that all citizens of America have the knowledge to access those entities when they need to as adults. This will be a difficult task but one that the educational system can conquer.

Chapter 7

Teacher Tenure

"Do what is right for the artist and in turn that decision will be right for you."

~Irving Azarr, Rock and Roll Hall of Fame speech

One of the key hotspots in education is teacher tenure. This subject has been contentious in the past, with advocates for limiting tenure postulating a need to identify the effectiveness of a teacher by a singular measurement. In California, the examples would be the California High School Exit Exam (CAHSEE) and the Smarter Balanced Assessment Consortium (SBAC). To be clear, tenure is a necessary component of education; however, the variables needed to educate a child are so vast that a person's livelihood should not be taken away based on a singular measure.

Many children will experience things in their lives that will inhibit their success in school. Children lose family members. They can become gravely ill themselves. Parental issues of absences, poverty, criminal influence, and other societal distractions detract from education. These are just some external possibilities that can devastate any student along their educational journey. This does not include the countless mental and relational battles that each student struggles with each moment. And this was all before cell phones with cameras and social media, which exposes them to even more esteem-crushing experiences.

Society does not imprison the parents of a child who doesn't eat their vegetables, and a teacher should not be fired because a student refuses to work. That being stated, teachers should not be immune from being held accountable for poor performance. If the reimagining of education is to take hold, teachers unions must be open to some reconceptualization as well. So the question arises, how do you truly measure a teacher's effectiveness and evaluate their performance?

The answer lies in the ability for the current system to be changed in a manner that keeps teachers accountable while protecting them from disinformation, personal management bias, and factors outside their control. A new step-by-step process utilizing current teaching standards benefits teachers who are tenured as well as probationary. This structure will allow teachers to feel safe in their work while continuing to be held accountable. Teachers will be motivated to perform and will be challenged to explore new avenues of the teaching craft, which, in turn, benefits students.

For most school districts, the current system of tenure is structured as a long probation period, similar to any other job. Teachers are hired as "probationary" and must be repeatedly observed using the agreed-upon standards of teaching. Each year there is feedback given to the teacher during post-observation meetings, with opportunities to show improvement. This process continues for an agreed number of years—two years in my district—until the teacher is granted tenure. From that moment on, teachers are virtually immune from termination, with few exceptions. Teachers can perform, or not, for years without accountability. Ultimately, thousands of children can be hindered when a poorly performing teacher is allowed to stay in place for a number of years. This situation has devastating consequences for the school, the district, the teaching profession, and the future.

The innovative change would take the following steps:

1. Teacher probationary periods would be doubled to four years prior to granting tenure.

This will allow educational leaders to really mentor and work with newly hired teachers to improve their methods. Training and college courses could be used to support and expand that teacher's expertise in the profession. The probationary period would change to a mentorship program where the candidate would be evaluated on overall performance within every element of a school culture. Tenure would become a semi-permanent fit within a school community, and the evaluation should be the same.

2. Teacher tenure should be re-evaluated every six years.

Most current systems evaluate teachers every other year on a couple standards. If the evaluation is negative, they are generally given an improvement plan to be implemented in the areas of concern. The challenge to this method is when the administrative team changes during the time of the teacher's process of improvement. Or the plan is not given the important focus because of the overworked administrator and summarily disappears. There are occasions when multiple plans are used but are never litigated because of the money necessary for prosecution. This leaves large areas of need—and sometimes, neglect—unchecked within the educational system.

To be clear, most teachers are consummate professionals who work themselves to the bone every day to positively influence the future by motivating kids to learn. Not all teachers are detrimental to students, but there is the potential for student detriment in the current tenure model. It is baked in the cake. No teachers union is going to say they want to represent teachers who hurt kids. Their responsibility lies in protecting teachers from being mistreated. Teachers generally believe there should be more accountability among their ranks for teachers who do not teach well. Teachers unions want as much accountability for teaching as everyone else. That is, until one of their members is accused of mistreating students in some fashion or being stagnant in their methods. Their situation is precarious because they are also responsible for defending these individuals. The most lucrative system of fairness is to have all feedback aspects of teaching be utilized during the tenure evaluation.

The craft of teaching is an evolutionary process like any other career. I am reminded of some experiences in the technology industry. People were educated in college to get a high-paying job in the area of computer coding that was the most cutting edge when they graduated. The problem, however, is that coding changes at lightning speed, which requires these people to constantly learn new languages to maintain their viability. If they don't, they are left with a buggy bumper industry and discarded like a VHS tape. (Yes, some of us are that old.) Similar to computer coding, the teaching profession must constantly evolve with new pedagogy, curriculum, technology, standards, testing methods, and every other element in the classroom. If the teacher refuses to become the lifelong learner they proselytize, they should be held accountable.

A new innovation would be keeping the same system with some modifications. Teachers would be evaluated every other year on standards assigned by the administrator rather than the tradition of agreeing on a couple of them. Under the new system, the teacher's tenure would be open for review every six years. The entire school is periodically evaluated by an accreditation board, so the process should be similar for the instruction within the school.

This every-six-year tenure evaluation would be administered via a multi-tiered system. Two observations would be conducted by the current school site administration on all teaching standards. Data would converge into the traditional end-of-year evaluation. The change comes when this evaluation is added to a tenure audit process, which looks at the overall effectiveness of the teacher. The tenure audit would be conducted by a panel that would include:

◊ District administrator
◊ School site administrator
◊ Teachers Union representative
◊ Classified Union representative
◊ Community person

One additional element is that the evaluation would be done blindly by the state. The county office of education would offer the evaluation information to the committees, which would be blinded. Materials submitted to the committee would include:

◊ the observations from the last issuance of tenure
◊ a human resources summary of standing from the teacher's personnel file
◊ testaments from current and past students and parents

◊ input from department chairs and fellow department members

◊ input from classified personnel

This committee would look over the material provided on the evaluation to determine interventions necessary for teacher improvement. This would then result one of the following:

◊ Clear renewal of tenure

◊ Maintain tenure with improvement in certain identified areas

◊ Return to a probationary status with an improvement plan

◊ Revocation of tenure with ability to terminate

The benefits of this system are the fairness of the evaluation and the ability to make it as objective as possible. The depth of information will paint the comprehensive profile of the teacher and their current status in the profession. The blind examination limits bias beyond any current community relationships or grievances. Evaluation teams are a true collective group that represents the community. Finally, the team's decision is free from the mountain of litigation and resources it generally takes to remove a tenured teacher who is truly not performing. Most importantly, this system can provide accountability and support for teachers to continually strive for their own success as professionals.

This new program holds teachers accountable to the profession they have voluntarily chosen to assign themselves to. History has shown that people generally take the path of least resistance, and teacher tenure has shown this to be true. The review of tenure can generate continual conversations about the visions and goals each teacher must regenerate to progress in their professional development. With time, a generation of teachers will emerge who are self-driven to constantly explore new areas of improvement with a consequential component for added motivation. Let all educators embrace the commitment of embodying the lifelong learners they prescribe and be the professionals they should be.

Chapter 8

Leveraging Technology

Technology is a continually evolving entity within the educational environment. It seems that every year brings a myriad of improvements teachers must immediately master for student achievement. The COVID-19 pandemic has shown, for example, that the direct relationship between newly adopted technology (virtual meetings) and learning is very limited because personal connections are not developed. Teachers struggle to create that link for their students. This monumental task being added to the other multitudes of responsibilities of teachers throughout every single day produces inconsistencies. The implementation of these new technologies has such a wide range of success and failure that the districts are uncertain of the actual impact of the technology on student learning.

By focusing staff to this purpose, each teacher can take the necessary time to fully educate and incorporate the technology at its maximum level into the learning experience. The use of the technology in a collective framework or body of work allows students to benefit with the clearest resource throughout their educational experience. The COVID-19 pandemic has forced teachers to learn how to embody most aspects of teaching within a virtual world. Although the collegiate experience has been experimenting with this new form of teaching throughout the last decade, the K-12 system is still in its infancy in adapting these technologies for the benefit of their population. As the saying goes, "A user interface is like a joke. If you have to explain it, it's not that good." (Martin Leblanc)

Once the issue of technology is resolved, the craft of teaching can then focus on what the student is receiving and not what the teacher is communicating. True analysis of the many assessment reports within the technological platforms—i.e., websites teachers utilize—can be consumed and used to influence future lessons. Teachers will be able to evaluate the success of engagement through the amount of time each student interfaces or the use of certain resources within the virtual environment. Those elements that are not utilized can then be evaluated and investigated for possible miscommunications and other issues that could inhibit their effectiveness.

PLCs will benefit from the multitude of discussions generated in how students experience the virtual portions of learning, along with the resources in the education. To put it more plainly, teachers will be able to explore and maximize technology in a cohesive manner for the students' learning experience. The result will be an effortless integration of behavioral reflection within skills-based learning.

Textbook publishers have focused a lot of attention in this area in order to generate results in the blink of an eye. Question banks are offered with predetermined questions which focus on the approved curriculums. Summative forms of assessments are offered with flexibility for the teacher to tailor the assessment to the lesson objectives. Results and analysis of the assessment data are instantaneous to a granular level. These tools are amazing because a teacher does not have to generate tests every week. However, the current educational system does not provide the time necessary to maximize these tools. Although these new features are good, they are underutilized because the initial focus of how the technology is developed is not innovative. The publishers did not adapt their technology to school needs but just transcribed their curriculums from print to digital in order to keep overhead down. True innovation would start with the premise that students can access anything they need for learning, and the teacher's purpose is solely to support the exploration. Instead of forcing the students to read a certain type of information, they should be creating a network of resources for mastering the standards.

Many times, the publishers provide one or two types of questions for a standard with the stipulation that the teacher has the "flexibility" to generate their own. The challenge in putting that into practice is that teachers need a minimum of four or five different questions for multiple achievement levels (easy, moderate, hard) to address each standard. Absences, administrative interruptions, parent meetings, and students just having an off day are some of the challenges every teacher faces in providing an assessment. And these situations assume that students will not try to work the system in order to get a better grade. These situations require focused attention on test generation and flexibility so that students are truly assessed in the best possible manner. Assessment is more than generating questions and having students perform. It is engaging students where they are. Creating test questions focused on possible career pathways or interests will engage students to strive for better success and ease because of the confidence they have in the subject without thinking about the question at hand.

Leveraging the tools of technology for the best experience of students will make learning individual, interesting, engaging, and (frankly) fun.

Section 5

Rebuilding the Castle

Then the reconstruction would begin, with some structures being completely different constructions from the previous. Others were erected with similar structures as the previous but with modifications that made the castle better.

So far we have deconstructed the educational experience, found the prime directive, and reorganized the classroom experience. But education does not occur in a bubble, and the consideration of the entire school site must be included. In any new venture, implementation planning must be considered in the restructuring of the program; however, all things must focus on the prime directive. Crucial to any implementation plan is the understanding of how the population will react. Some ideas in this section are in direct contradiction of institutional traditions that all stakeholders have come to enjoy. Unfortunately, these traditions do not help students get the required learning. These following ideas are offered with the mindset of the needs of education for students and the opportunities for students to simultaneously contribute to society.

Chapter 9

School Calendar

For years, a number of scholars have advocated for changing the school calendar to reflect more of a business-oriented schedule rather than an agrarian schedule as depicted in Figure 3. The argument for this change in tradition is based on the fact that the advanced industrial society does not reflect a seasonal need. This calendar change has been proven in a number of charter schools to be somewhat successful. As more political pressure is being applied to adopt a new calendar that expands the school year, districts and states must find a plan that can incorporate a number of aspects. Teachers unions and child advocates are against a year-round schedule because it seems to overload the student. The pressures of learning on a consistent basis have proven to be detrimental to the emotional state of students. Additionally, teachers, administrators, and school site workers will state there is a direct need for students and teachers to separate themselves periodically in order to readjust the learning environment back to zero. Most school districts have the longest stretch of instruction between the beginning of school and Thanksgiving break. Data has shown that around the beginning of October, school discipline referrals start to increase. The referral types are mainly based on defiance, disruption to the learning environment, and ignoring directives. These micro issues can be adjusted with this new framework while maintaining a high level of education. The key to this situation is changing the calendar.

Many different options have been provided to districts for them to map a calendar that meets the needs of their local community.

Whether that is the beginning of school time, the number of hours in school, or the flexibility of those timeframes within classes, each community has a separate need based on the number of influences within the area. Each community must traverse many obstacles to serve their stakeholders. These needs can be different, depending on the community. Rural agricultural students have different transportation needs than those in dense cities. No matter what the impetus, the school calendar should reflect the needs of the community it serves. It is for this reason that this particular writing will not advocate for a specific school calendar. However, moving away from the traditional, semester-based process with a "break" is necessary to increase the level of intellect of our students. So how do districts incorporate a school calendar that effectively educates students while giving them enough time off from the learning environment to reset? This essential question must be addressed by the specific district.

The solution can be varied, based on those needs. A semester process with an inclusion of a small, intensive summer school component can be an effective process. Some school districts have moved into a trimester process where they split the calendar in thirds with a month—or three-week—break between the trimesters for students to "reboot." An additional option would be to separate the school calendar from January to January into five segments. Each section would be comprised of a nine-week instructional term, with a one-week break between each segment, as shown in Figure 4. Finally, a four-section option would provide 11 weeks of instruction per segment (depicted in Figure 5). As stated previously, these are only ideas; individual communities must decide the structure that best serves their stakeholders.

62 William G. Cloo Ed.D.

Figure 3: Traditional School Calendar

January						
S	M	T	W	T	F	S
			1	2	3	4
5	6	7	8	9	10	11
12	13	14	15	16	17	18
19	20	21	22	23	24	25
26	27	28	29	30	31	

February						
S	M	T	W	T	F	S
						1
2	3	4	5	6	7	8
9	10	11	12	13	14	15
16	17	18	19	20	21	22
23	24	25	26	27	28	29

March						
S	M	T	W	T	F	S
1	2	3	4	5	6	7
8	9	10	11	12	13	14
15	16	17	18	19	20	21
22	23	24	25	26	27	28
29	30	31				

April						
S	M	T	W	T	F	S
		1	2	3	4
5	6	7	8	9	10	11
12	13	14	15	16	17	18
19	20	21	22	23	24	25
26	27	28	29	30		

May						
S	M	T	W	T	F	S
					1	2
3	4	5	6	7	8	9
10	11	12	13	14	15	16
17	18	19	20	21	22	23
24	25	26	27	28	29	30
31						

June						
S	M	T	W	T	F	S
1	2	3	4	5	6
7	8	9	10	11	12	13
14	15	16	17	18	19	20
21	22	23	24	25	26	27
28	29	30				

July						
S	M	T	W	T	F	S
			1	2	3	4
5	6	7	8	9	10	11
12	13	14	15	16	17	18
19	20	21	22	23	24	25
26	27	28	29	30	31	

August						
S	M	T	W	T	F	S
						1
2	3	4	5	6	7	8
9	10	11	12	13	14	15
16	17	18	19	20	21	22
23	24	25	26	27	28	29
30	31					

September						
S	M	T	W	T	F	S
		1	2	3	4	5
6	7	8	9	10	11	12
13	14	15	16	17	18	19
20	21	22	23	24	25	26
27	28	29	30			

October						
S	M	T	W	T	F	S
				1	2	3
4	5	6	7	8	9	10
11	12	13	14	15	16	17
18	19	20	21	22	23	24
25	26	27	28	29	30	31

November						
S	M	T	W	T	F	S
1	2	3	4	5	6	7
8	9	10	11	12	13	14
15	16	17	18	19	20	21
22	23	24	25	26	27	28
29	30					

December						
S	M	T	W	T	F	S
		1	2	3	4	5
6	7	8	9	10	11	12
13	14	15	16	17	18	19
20	21	22	23	24	25	26
27	28	29	30	31		

- Holidays

Figure 4: 5-Section School Calendar (2021-22)

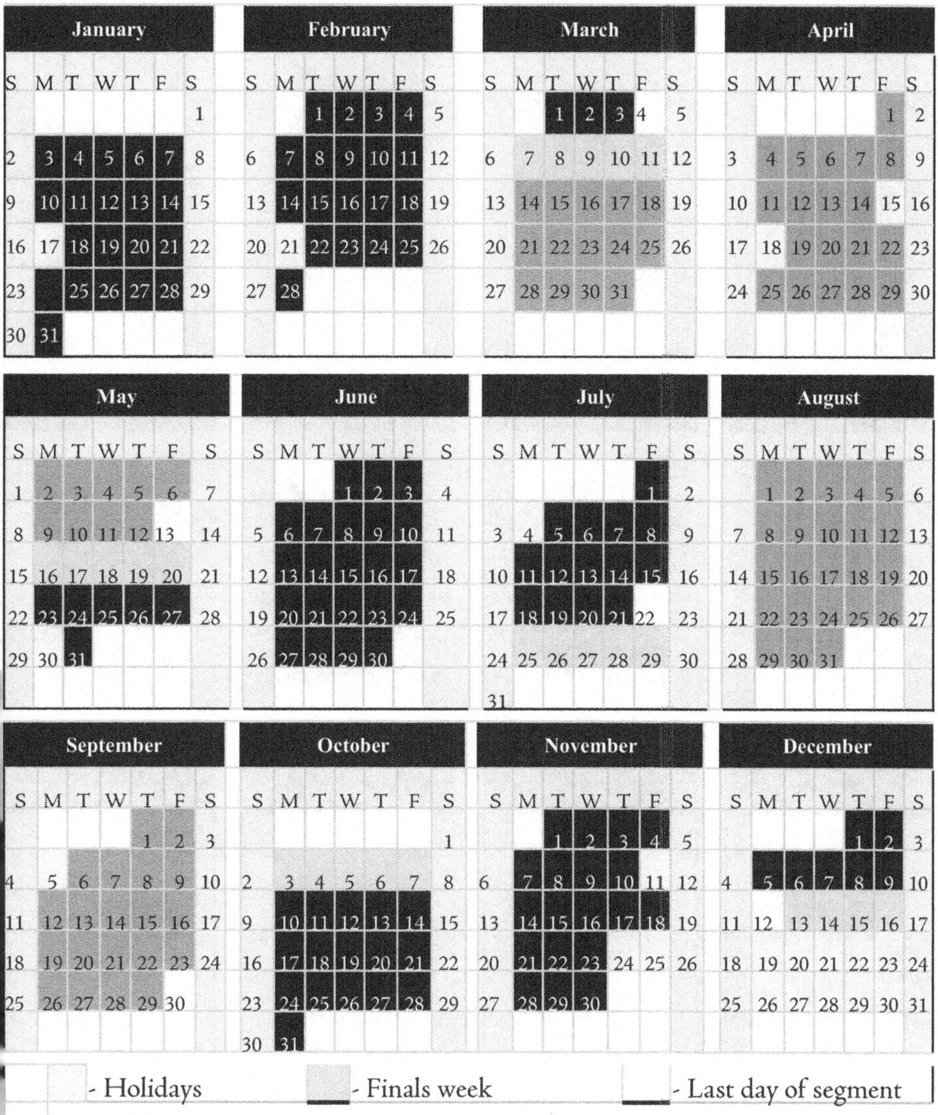

- Holidays   - Finals week   - Last day of segment

Days Available – 241

Finals week- 20

Total instruction days – 221 (1 Float holiday)

Instructional Days per section – 43

William G. Cloo Ed.D.

Figure 5: 4-Section School Calendar (2021-22)

January								February								March								April						
S	M	T	W	T	F	S		S	M	T	W	T	F	S		S	M	T	W	T	F	S		S	M	T	W	T	F	S
						1				1	2	3	4	5				1	2	3	4	5							1	2
2	3	4	5	6	7	8		6	7	8	9	10	11	12		6	7	8	9	10	11	12		3	4	5	6	7	8	9
9	10	11	12	13	14	15		13	14	15	16	17	18	19		13	14	15	16	17	18	19		10	11	12	13	14	15	16
16	17	18	19	20	21	22		20	21	22	23	24	25	26		20	21	22	23	24	25	26		17	18	19	20	21	22	23
23	24	25	26	27	28	29		27	28							27	28	29	30	31				24	25	26	27	28	29	30
30	31																													

May								June								July								August						
S	M	T	W	T	F	S		S	M	T	W	T	F	S		S	M	T	W	T	F	S		S	M	T	W	T	F	S
1	2	3	4	5	6	7					1	2	3	4							1	2		1	2	3	4	5	6
8	9	10	11	12	13	14		5	6	7	8	9	10	11		3	4	5	6	7	8	9		7	8	9	10	11	12	13
15	16	17	18	19	20	21		12	13	14	15	16	17	18		10	11	12	13	14	15	16		14	15	16	17	18	19	20
22	23	24	25	26	27	28		19	20	21	22	23	24	25		17	18	19	20	21	22	23		21	22	23	24	25	26	27
29	30	31						26	27	28	29	30				24	25	26	27	28	29	30		28	29	30	31			
																31														

September								October								November								December						
S	M	T	W	T	F	S		S	M	T	W	T	F	S		S	M	T	W	T	F	S		S	M	T	W	T	F	S
				1	2	3								1			1	2	3	4	5					1	2	3
4	5	6	7	8	9	10		2	3	4	5	6	7	8		6	7	8	9	10	11	12		4	5	6	7	8	9	10
11	12	13	14	15	16	17		9	10	11	12	13	14	15		13	14	15	16	17	18	19		11	12	13	14	15	16	17
18	19	20	21	22	23	24		16	17	18	19	20	21	22		20	21	22	23	24	25	26		18	19	20	21	22	23	24
25	26	27	28	29	30			23	24	25	26	27	28	29		27	28	29	30					25	26	27	28	29	30	31
								30	31																					

- Holidays
- Finals week
- Last day of segment

Days Available – 241

Finals week- 20

Total instruction days 221 (1 Float holiday)

Instructional Days per section. 55

Most calendars have the student as the center of the calendar creation. The student is the product and the sole purpose of the school, and it is right that calendars be created for that purpose. However, engrained within this system is the required health and motivation of the teacher to achieve the highest learning performance. It is within this avenue that the framework established in this book can assist. At the discretion of the district and stakeholders, they can choose to have teachers take one, six-week sabbatical in order for them to be able to reboot, re-teach, learn, take a class, or go on vacation. Another avenue could be that teachers would rotate the roles of the framework in order for them to have an offsite experience to spend more time with their families. For example, perhaps a teacher is a presenter (a role outlined later in this book) for five of the seven teaching segments but then steps back to the developer role, which is not directly related to students. This role can be done remotely from anywhere in the world. Struggling teachers could be directed to a sabbatical for professional development in order to maintain their performance. The premise of this process is that by supporting the growth and wellbeing of the teachers, the craft of teaching will not become stagnant.

These calendars can also provide benefits for district goals and projects. Districts could mandate that certain segments of teachers step back completely from teaching for a six-week, intensive of one specific teaching methodology, pedagogy, or other teaching processes. New initiatives can begin with real training practices as intensives rather than one-day workshops. Training on focused curriculum advancement is perpetuated on a continual basis so that the district truly provides a well-trained professional learning procedure that can be articulated by both students and teachers alike. District-wide task forces can be created to collaborate on program changes, which can foster the talents of all the staff to innovate school systems.

The calendar reinforces the flexibility needed for specific school site needs or if a new emergency materializes. Pandemics, weather occurrences, or societal stressors can cause schools to change the school experiences. These calendars allow for small, negative impacts to occur while the students' overall learning continues. An example is the hybrid class model. Should the need arise, different class cohorts could access the campus at specific times. The flow of students onto the campus at any one time would be less than the total number of students who are enrolled on the campus, which could keep people safe. The calendar can limit the needs of facilities for necessary repairs. Staggered vacations can create space on the campus. For example, the ninth-grade vacation could be from the end of April to the end of May, which would allow the upperclassman to really recognize and celebrate the graduating class as they travel on to graduation ceremonies without impeding upon the educational experience. The opportunities are endless in the ability for people to transfer those different components in extension or contraction of the educational experience to better suit the stakeholder consistency within any school site.

This calendar framework provides the flexibility and opportunity necessary for reimagining course offerings and extension processes for all students. Additionally, it allows for the flexibility of interventions and large levels of success for all students. An added benefit is the ability for teachers, staff, and students to be able to vacation whenever they might need. Family emergencies or sickness might arise, which allows teachers to extend their sabbatical time to a seven-week process. This would allow a district to truly show their support for their stakeholders during their most desperate times of need.

Calendar Considerations

One of the key arguments against this kind of structure is the speed at which these sections of instruction are to be given. Teachers could argue that they cannot compact an entire semester of instruction into a nine-week section. An innovative solution would be that each semester would incorporate two instructional segments, which would then increase the time frame to an 18-week segment. Most teachers would agree that losing two to four weeks of instruction could be doable in most cases. A benefit of this structure would be more opportunities to assess student progress by providing more moments to trigger a schedule change for struggling or excelling students. The performance-based, vertical articulation of students can be increased in a smaller capacity. Additionally, the master schedule allows students the opportunity to graduate faster, based on their performance. If a specific student cohort is lacking the mastery of certain standards or skills, repeat classes with different teacher teams could be established in order to address those issues. Additionally, class offerings could be postponed for a seven-week term in order for the team to really concentrate on reestablishing the needs of those students and evaluating the effectiveness of the instruction, with the understanding that they would re-engage with those students in the next term.

The advanced placement program has always been an advantage to a certain subsection of students within any school community. These students are given a greater level of rigor that incorporates not only the regular standards of any student but also the extension lessons necessary to succeed at a collegiate level. The assessment for this program is the advanced placement test that is given every spring. Under the current structure, the advanced placement courses established for the lower grades provide an undue burden of establishing student writing proficiency along with challenging content in order for students' scores to be very high. This burden is lightened as the student progressively experiences more advanced placement classes throughout their high school careers—e.g., calculus, statistics, psychology, Spanish literature, computer science—all having the privilege of being built on the established foundation of writing given at the lower grades. The contradictory problem is that students might think they are not successful in the advanced placement program because of their lack of knowledge when the real reason could be their incomplete writing abilities.

Advanced placement curriculum classes could be regenerated as an elective (as it is listed in the master schedule) without the added component of the specific subject matter. The advanced placement program could include a mandatory foundational writing course so that the students could have a basic writing component that is more advanced for the testing process. All other advanced placement courses would then concentrate on their advanced subject matter, again being electives, for the passing of their subject matter tests. Review lessons could be conducted from the base foundational writing course necessary for success. By supporting a true writing curriculum as a prerequisite to any test that might be given at the subject matter, these struggles can be addressed in a more supportive environment. Again, the foundational basis of this new teaching framework is the state fiduciary responsibility that the high school has to prepare their students for graduation at the high school level, with collegiate acceptance being an added benefit.

Calendar Benefits

The new style of calendars presents a more comprehensive experience for students, which reflects an adult life. Additionally, the new calendars provide flexibility for stakeholders, based on the needs of the school and the student. Families will not have to choose between the longer vacation or family reunion and school. Students could represent the country in the Winter Olympics without any academic fallout. Teachers and staff members could truly gain professional development from educational institutions outside their local area. Finally, if some unforeseen physical or mental injury occurs, the school can support them through those tough times. All these experiences convey compassion and support at a real level.

Chapter 10

The School Day

Traditional School Day

This new innovation does require that education take a step back in order to maximize the necessary components for success. A block schedule must be reinstated by the school for students to maximize their time on campus. One of the largest challenges for students with block scheduling is that teachers make the assumption that off-day school blocks were to be filled with instructional minutes. This overwhelms students and leads to fewer successes. Some schools have been able to find the necessary components for block scheduling to make it an effective process, and those resources should be maximized to the best success of the school.

Shifting to a block-schedule week will allow students to fit within a societal process whereby they will be able to maximize their college transition, entry-level job experience, or any other endeavor. The block scheduling process will also make it easier for parents to commit to transportation processes and make a stable environment for their high school children, moving forward. One of the largest issues with most high schools is that there is a saturation point for students in academic classes after the 12 o'clock lunch. Academic fatigue can set in, which is reflected in the grades of classes in the later periods. Most counselors try their best to put academic classes within the first four periods of the school day as much as possible, with types of support classes being scheduled for the afternoons.

The challenge with this process is that students will not be able to excel in these academic classes after noon because of the saturation point.

Figure 6 outlines the necessary components for a student to be successful in graduation using the block-schedule, traditional-setting model. Again, graduation requirements are the only consideration for high schools, and the following Figure 7 outlines how a student can be completely matriculated within block periods. Intervention classes and remediation classes can be offered as electives at the end of the day so that students could receive the necessary interventions without slowing their chances for graduation.

Figure 6: Student Experience for Graduation

9th	10th	11th	12th
Block A English	Block A Math	Block A English	Block A Math
Block B Visual / Performing Art	Block B Government	Block B History	Block B Hist Elective / Economics
Math	Elective	Math	Elective
Science	Science	Science	Foreign Language

Figure 7: Traditional Block School Day

Monday	Tuesday	Wednesday	Thursday	Friday
Block A English	Block A Math	Block A English	Block A Math	Students: Input day (Attendance by download access) Teachers: PLC Grading Meetings
Block B History	Block B Science	Block B History	Block B Science	
Elective	Elective	Elective	Elective	
Elective	Elective	Elective	Elective	

The above structure is just as flexible as any other component outlined within this book. The purpose of the above graphs is to illustrate the ability for the students to gain the necessary graduation requirements within the four periods outlined in a block schedule. Sequencing of these particular classes is completely at the discretion of the district representatives and counselors in creating the master schedule. But the classification of designating certain classes by grade level must be examined. Education needs to be accessible to all grades within the current standards structure. This will allow for a wider range of experience for students and a more tailored education. For example, some students could take art during their ninth-grade year for their fine art requirement because they wish to pursue that passion, while others might take government/economics during ninth grade because they wish to become a lawyer or politician.

Some classes are designed for a much more mature audience of upperclassman. Schools should reevaluate the curriculums of these particular courses so they are wide enough for all students, regardless of class cohort. The result is an educational experience that reflects the acumen of the student and their desired aspirations to other institutions or workplaces.

Another myth that is addressed within the traditional-day school model is the necessity that the school needs to become a cultural home for all its students. Admittedly, a lot of our students do not have a place of safety or individual expression for them to adopt the societal norms that are necessary for success in a mature society. This structure does provide for that to continue; however, it is not the basis for how the school is structured. The prime directive of providing students the necessary classes for high school graduation is the only cornerstone by which this block schedule is created. Local and state governments must provide the other structures. The transportation department does not provide private drivers for the elderly, and the school should not take the role of family counseling or police. Schools could be a location for these entities to access students and collectively support the community.

An example is the food distribution of schools to poorer families. The facilities, food, and staff are in place, but the coordination with other local agencies limits the program's success. If the local representative had offices on (or near) the campus to coordinate the program in a collective effort (budget, et al.), the program could reach more of the needed population. Another example would be that family therapy support groups could be held on the campus so families would have easier access to these services. COVID-19 has created a large need for grief counseling and mental health services, and the local community should support those services.

It should be noted that the school would be staying within the prime directive. The outside entities would use the school location as a support system for their responsibilities. The school would not be coordinating or responsible for the services beyond the use of its facilities; however, families would see the school as a place of support or comfort.

Additionally, schools need to be honest with themselves in understanding how electives are maintained within their classrooms and school cultures. All current electives are created and maintained through the extraordinary efforts of the teachers who teach them. That is indisputable. Electives are not even created, much less offered, unless a teacher generates the curricula and it is accepted by the district—and possibly a college board. Those electives are then branded and marketed for student interest. Electives are maintained if the student interest is cultivated and the benefit of that elective is continually proven to the school community. Year after year, the funding must be fought over, and most times that funding is not given. It is only the tenacity of the teacher to do something they love that yields student electives. Unfortunately, the educational institutions must understand that electives are as their name says—something above and beyond the central core curriculum of the school's purpose. Although it is a nice thing to do, electives cannot supersede the graduation of the student.

Some feedback regarding this new framework structure would be that some teachers, who are specialists in a specific elective, would then not be able to have a complete contract or contribute except in the afternoons. This actually is false. As outlined in the different positions within the innovative framework, a number of teachers from different disciplines could actually influence the key four subjects of English, math, science, and history. More school districts have leveraged their hiring power to ensure that teachers in their employ are able to directly impact core classrooms, with electives being a secondary process. Teachers would be encouraged to expand their credential processes to one of the key four curriculums, but they could also contribute to the current structure of the learning environment through the secondary processes and support structures of the new innovative framework (i.e., developer or interventionist).

For example, foreign language teachers could assist with the intervention of grammar structures or vocabulary words. Physical education teachers could assist with mathematics and/or science in terms of interventions for procedures, direction following, and multiple-step equations. Please note, this would only be for teachers who do not already have a secondary specialty in a core subject.

The necessity of time for teachers to truly collaborate in all facets of the learning experience must be a key component, which is why the school week is only four days long. The traditional school-bell schedule provided the opportunity for teachers to collaborate in a continual process, as outlined in the previous chapters. A truly collaborative environment on Friday would allow teachers the consistency of reflection and planning. The purpose for these meetings would be to identify successes and updates of the learning process for all students within their class team. The next purpose would be to generate innovative plans and interventions to continually improve the curriculum. Short-term and long-term goals would be identified and evaluated on a continual basis. Updates and feedback from all members of the team would be shared so that every aspect of the learning experience would be available to the team.

The Friday experience for students would be an input day of concepts and terminology for the upcoming week in all their classes. Students would see lectures on key concepts in a screen-cast or video process, and they could review those as many times as needed. Checking for understanding, note taking, discussions, and other forms of formative assessment can be conducted with these presentation processes. Students will be provided the opportunity to prove their understanding of the concepts, thereby ensuring the learning process for instructional minutes. The three-day weekend for students will allow parents the chance to make the necessary travel plans they usually need around certain holidays and limit the risk of absences within the school day. Because learning is an asynchronous process for all students, it can be conducted in any manner as long as there is Wi-Fi.

The mindset for lesson planning needs to shift toward a stu-dent-centered support role. The "classroom" has the reputation of being the teacher's domain, where they are the ruler of everything that is conducted during their allotted time. This model works for the students who have the tactical knowledge to traverse this obstacle course of learning. The understanding to "keep your head down and mouth shut" gains a positive reputation with the teacher. Students must create their own network of tutors within the class period or subject in order to generate a foundation of support for their success. This resourcefulness is revered in educational circles in preparing them for leadership roles that build teams for achieve-ment. Students can wrestle with this model when they grapple with independence or are confused by certain concepts.

However, whether it is introversion or pride, the many struggles that prevent students from reaching out, so they do not suffer the humiliation of "not knowing," dramatically hinders many students. The shy student who does not ask questions is lost and could fail the assessment on the concept. The year of COVID-19 has proven the lack of grit and motivation of students. When left for themselves, most crumble under the isolation and pressure. Interestingly, this has always happened, but it was in the first year of college. So the educational community could wash their hands of the situation with the ideas "they weren't ready" or "the workforce would be better." Now, the number of kids who have failed in the 2020-21 school year shows the need for instructing students (and parents) with the tools of self-motivation.

Teacher credential programs have started to address this issue with a new cohort of teachers who are focused on student interventions from a theory perspective. Unfortunately, the system they are brought into does not assist with the continuation of this mindset. The Friday collaborations within the new framework allow for this process to be maximized. The mindset of class time on the campus must shift to the idea of "learning resources" for student achievement. This new structure allows the school staff to guide the student to be responsible and seek out the necessary resources for their success. Current levels of student engagement in the learning process must be evaluated, and deficits must be addressed. Most importantly, students can be celebrated for reaching out and attaining their accomplishments.

Remember, lesson presentations are provided virtually to all students. This allows the student to view the material from home on Fridays under the new bell schedule, with the added benefit of repeated viewing at their discretion. On-campus time allocation will shift to intervention and clarification during the allotted campus classroom time. Students engage in the learning process by articulating their own needs at the beginning of class time. Activities for the students are based on the needs of the student; however, certain elements of the learning will be established as baseline activities for any unit.

◊ Multiple formative assessment opportunities
◊ Metacognitive reflection and exploration of handling new learning
◊ Team-oriented product processes
◊ Practice time with the concept in real-world applications
◊ Self-organization and planning time to maximize work and learning

Please note that these activities are just some of the kaleidoscope of experiences students could have with the ingenuity of the teacher team. The key element is that true student-driven learning is occurring with teachers guiding the student in the learning process. Additionally, struggles—or in some cases denial—of work will be highlighted, with opportunities for parent involvement and reinforcement of student success.

It is completely understandable for educators to feel real trepidation with the student having this much choice in their learning. We are asking teachers to conduct classes without being prepared for the class time. How will administrators know they are teaching? The first indicator is the need for the teacher desk to disappear. In a learning-resource format, there is no need for a teacher to sit in most cases. Monitoring would occur instantaneously by clarifying directions and consistently inquiring on the next steps for the student to continue.

The agenda of every class period would remain somewhat similar to what has been communicated for the last 20 years. Clear standards and objectives must be visible for resources and reinforcements. A set of goals for the unit must be visible for students to evaluate their position in the learning progression and plan accordingly. Deadlines for assessments and student work must be posted for reference. The structure is provided for students to succeed, with the available resources to support their learning. It is in the "how" of the learning process that students will find a new way of doing things. This structure allows for students to create their own assessments tailored to their own interests and dreams. Assessments created by the teacher teams should be open enough for students to use resource materials of their choice.

Student reluctance can be addressed with students engaging in the learning process every day instead of when they are convinced to take a certain class. Comments of, "There are classes you are just not going to want to do," should be signals for teams to change the engagement of the curriculum. Teacher-student trust will need to be constantly established every single day. These challenges are hard but worth it. Teachers reflect that, "My kids were great this year." How wonderful could it be if their kids were the whole school.

What could it look like in a classroom?

A standard day is hard to visualize within the new framework. The rhythm of teaching starts on the previous week instead of on Monday. For example, if classes were to address the standard of understanding grade-level text during the modern period of literature, the unit would start on a Friday with an overview of the unit during the input phase. A list of requirements for showing mastery would be communicated, with multiple opportunities for completing them. The assessments would give opportunities for students to explore the questions they might have regarding this age. Perhaps a family biography project that explains how their families dealt with the Great Depression that compares with stories from the resource list. Or an investigative project as to how the stock market really collapsed in the United States. Additionally, a required resource list would be provided to students to use for reading. Other concepts in grammar, vocabulary development, and literary analysis would be provided digitally to the students for their reference at any time.

On-campus class-period agendas are depicted graphically in Figure 8. It starts with a review and confirmation of the standard that needs to be addressed that day, along with a review of the assessment. Next, a small reflection time is conducted for the student to evaluate their position in the learning journey, which is communicated (physically or digitally) to the teacher. Next, the work begins. Students engage in the work and are required to show a concept map of their project, integration of grammar goals in the work, draft of the project, multiple feedback forms completed by peers, etc. These workings are monitored and checked, with teachers focusing student attention on the work and guided plans for achievement. The end of the period is marked by a reflective period on the student's accomplishment during class time and necessary things to focus on until the next meeting. A crucial element is an emphasis for the student to explore "how" they worked during the period. Did they maximize their time? Did they use all the resources they needed? Were they lost at any point on what to do and why? These reflections would be the requirement before the beginning of the next period so students develop work ethic goals in addition to the checklist of the work.

Figure 8: Class Period Model

Time	Section	Product
10 min	Standard Review / Reflection	Goal setting for class time.
10 min	Deadlines and Assessment Clarification	Shared understanding of requirements
60 min	Work time	Assessment product
10 min	End of class performance evaluation	Home work plan

Bell Schedule

The bell schedule outlined in Figure 9 shows the necessary movements of students within a regular school day. These timeframes are examples that offer a regular school day to function and do assume some tendencies. The schedule would only be employed if a pandemic or other type of limitation were on the campus. Pivotal to the success of this daily schedule is the maximization of every single minute for graduation requirement classes within the school year.

A typical school has 180 days of instruction. If the average class period is 55 minutes long every single day, that will yield 165 hours for teachers to conduct learning to mastery. That means every student (at every level) must travel through the learning process within the state standard framework and prove mastery in less than two months of on-the-job training. The key focus of the bell schedule is to maximize motivation while minimizing the number of distractions in any given day. Every teacher has always fought for every single minute because of this daunting task. There will be societal issues that might fly in the face of the schedule, which is why it is encouraged that the schedule be flexible enough for the student population in the area.

It is impossible to provide a schedule that is impervious to all distractions; however, eliminating the ones that the school can control will maximize learning. Perhaps an elective period can be established at the beginning of the day for those students who might have challenges getting to school by 7:45 or 8:00 a.m. The same could be done at the end of the day for those students who might need to hold a job or deal with situations at home. It can be possible to be flexible yet never deviate from the core principles of the prime directive for graduation.

Figure 9: New Daily Bell Schedule – All Students on Campus

Daily Schedule - All Students On Campus					
Block A	7:45- 9:45 a.m.	120 min	Block A	7:45-9:45 a.m.	120 min
Break	9:45 - 9:55 a.m.	10 min	Break	9:45-9:55 a.m.	10 min
Block B	10:00-12:00 p.m.	120 min	Block B	10:00-12:00 p.m.	120 min
Lunch 1	12:00 -12:35 p.m.	35 min	Clubs / Electives	12:05-12:50 p.m.	45 min
Clubs / Electives	12:40 -1:25 p.m.	45 min	Lunch 2	12:50-1:25 p.m.	35 min
Elective 1	1:30 - 2:15 p.m.	45 min	Elective 1	1:30-2:15 p.m.	45 min
Elective 2	2:20 - 3:05 p.m.	45 min	Elective 2	2:20-3:05 p.m.	45 min

The reasoning behind the two-lunch system is for the food services department to be able to feed a student population of approximately 2,800 people within the 90-minute timeframe. Staggering the timeframe of the different classes would allow for proper distribution, consumption, and cleanup of the necessary food product. It should be noticed that there is a class of clubs/electives during lunch. The strategic placement of this particular class within the school day is an effort to reinforce the school culture. Utilization of this time should be determined by the district and/or school site. This class could be utilized as a homeroom period for a study hall or other cultural support process.

Another method of utilization would be the inclusion of clubs within the elective offerings of the school catalog. For example, an actual curriculum of the Interact Club would allow for those students who wish to have their desires of serving their community legitimized and actually placed on the transcript for future jobs and/or colleges to reference. Time has shown that electives generally start out as clubs and then matriculate into the school catalog without eliminating the club. The club then becomes the deciding body for the associate student body in order for business to be conducted. However, most of these meetings are held outside the view of most of the students within the club. Students are given the choice of being in a club or time with their friends, and we all know what teenagers will most like choose. By placing the club within the elective catalog from the start, students would be taught how to not only continue and maintain their desired dreams and interests within their clubs but would also be able to understand and learn the necessary components of leadership, compromise, advocacy, and civil discourse that is necessary for any organization to continue.

Some readers might initially dismiss this new daily schedule model with the electives being in the afternoon. The argument generally sounds like, "We cannot have all students participating in PE during two periods. There is not enough room!" However, an administrator looking at a master schedule can see that those electives can encapsulate all students during those class periods, provided they are appropriately placed. Additionally, the added electives will build the room needed for all students.

The largest designation change would be the inclusion of advanced placement within the master schedule. Although advanced placement courses are within the department that the test is in, it is a voluntarily chosen elective by the students and the teacher, which designates it as an elective. Again, the central focus of the high school is for the students to be able to prove their acumen of the state requirements for high school graduation not acceptance to college. Placing the advanced placement program within the confines of the electives allows for the exposure and opportunity of those students to classes without the inadvertent isolation of one cohort of students away from the general populace.

Other programs, from Project Lead The Way (PLTW) to computer science classes, can additionally be placed within the elective process so students can have that exposure but stay within the school curriculum. An argument can be made that the student's aptitude exceeds the standard curriculum, which will be detrimental to the student's motivation of interest within that subject matter. That argument isn't completely accurate within the new framework because of the embedded extension lessons within the core curriculums.

Added to this list would be any dual-enrollment classes that are conducted on the campus. Placing these classes in the afternoon allows integration of college professors on the high school campus. Students could also travel to their local colleges, which expands the ability for students to experience classes in a more collegiate-style environment. Students traveling to the alternate college site could lower the population on the high school campus in the afternoon. It would also allow for schools to possibly integrate more effectively within the local junior college system through transportation to give students an actual college experience on a college campus. Students who generally would not think of going to college could have the necessary exposure through taking electives (PE, art appreciation, etc.), which could increase the pathways of the students.

This bell schedule has a positive effect on the school environment. Reiterating the inclusion of clubs and their benefits within the school culture during lunchtime is a great benefit for the school. Different events and information activities can be conducted during the lunches, with zero impact on the core curriculum classes. Additionally, the necessary school meetings for students can be conducted in the afternoons on a continual basis from the beginning of the school year. meetings can all be held during the elective times, with minimal impact on the four major disciplines. Examples of these meeting would be parent-teacher conferences, 504 meetings (covered under Section 504 of the Rehabilitation Act), and Individual Educational Plan (IEP) Pep rallies, assemblies, sports celebrations, invited speakers, and other district cultural celebrations can be done during these times without any impact on core minutes for student achievement.

Again, the schedule provided in Figure 9 is a suggestive process that is completely flexible within the priorities of the school district and/or school site. For example, the electives at the end of the day could be condensed into a single class period, thereby expanding the time for each elective. The varieties of this particular schedule are flexible enough for any school process. However, the central role of making sure the blocks in the beginning of the day encapsulate the central learning necessary for graduation from high school is paramount to this bell schedule.

Hybrid Model

The COVID-19 pandemic created anxiety for all elements of society. As January 1, 2021, approached, a new type of hope started to gain momentum. The emergency approval of vaccines started the discussions of how society could start transitioning back to life before the pandemic. The pandemic has forced people and businesses to redefine success, which affects the restart plans. The integration of meetings in a virtual space and the redefining of "workspace" have made businesses aware that they can still maintain a certain level of productivity while limiting overhead and allowing employees to work from home.

For years, businesses have weighed the costs and benefits of home-based work with no real data to base their decisions on because most industries were not willing to take the necessary risks in order to completely evaluate the idea. There was a time when family leave was a bilateral decision. Employees had to choose between their careers and their families. The trust necessary for companies to empower their workforces to work from home without direct oversight was an idea only in theory. COVID-19 has obviously placed this situation in the laps of most people by forcing this trust into the workplace. As American society begins this post-pandemic time, businesses have diverged in their plans. Some businesses have noticed lower productivity due to a lack of collaboration. Some have noticed little change in productivity and look forward to continuing the home workspace. Others have only focused on getting "back to normal." The type of industry has predominantly dictated the desired new workplace. Education has been no different than private enterprise with this situation.

The initial vaccines were limited to adults only and not recommended for adolescent students. Because education spans over 12 years of a student's life, it will be difficult for the educational institution to create a reopening plan that fits all students. High school is a more unique situation, given the amount of exposure every student has with others on the campus and the massive population of each school. If schools are limited in their ability to open for all students, each district will be left with difficult decisions. As time has progressed, a traditional model became viable for the 2021-22 school year. However, this might not be the only time that a catastrophic situation occurs, thereby forcing schools back into isolation. The school system must be prepared.

Stakeholders are realizing that virtual learning has not been as successful as traditional settings for a number of reasons. The 2020 school year found students floundering in school, not because they cannot learn the material but because of *how* they were motivated and engaged with the material.

Students give up easily without consistent redirection. They become overwhelmed with the workload because teachers don't repeatedly walk them through the work and cannot ensure effort. Some students find success in balancing the needs of the high school experience with new ventures. Do districts risk the education of some students over others by restricting certain grades to a virtual-only experience? How do we open schools?

The largest benefit for integrating a hybrid-school model is that it provides education and support in a balanced way while building student independence and motivation. The input presentations (i.e., lectures on new material) and resources for learning can be conducted in a virtual manner outside the school campus. This still remains the most optimal situation for students because they can gain access and repeat the information as many times as possible for repeated support. Assessments and projects should also exist in the virtual realm. Time on campus could be solely focused on clarification, modeling, and the practice of learning.

At this time, the largest challenge to this strategy is the ability for students to do nefarious collaboration or cheating. This situation can be prevented through the creation of skills-based exams and further cyber security measures within the learning platform. A key focus in the creation of this schedule is the concentration of resources solely on the fiduciary requirements for graduation—the prime directive.

Figure 10. Hybrid Bell Schedule

Daily Schedule - Hybrid Model		
Block A	7:45 - 9:45 a.m.	Grades 9 & 10
Break	9:45 - 9:55 a.m.	
Block B	10:00 - 12:00 p.m.	
Lunch 1 12:00 - 12:35 p.m.		
Egress of morning 12:35 - 1:00 p.m.		
Block A	1:30 - 3:30 p.m.	Grades 11 & 12
Break	3:30 - 3:55 p.m.	
Block B	4:00 - 6:00 p.m.	
Egress of Evening 6:00 - 6:30 p.m.		

Using the hybrid system would require that all elective classes be conducted in an online format. Innovating most of the electives into this model can still expose student interests into a number of avenues. Time restrictions become less of a problem. These classes can be more intensive within a smaller amount of time or could be created in a self-guided format. Most interest-driven experiences for adults are conducted in a self-guided manner during company training, and so could the student experience.

Why should the classroom experience be any different from classes the students are interested in? The time restrictions of in-class instruction can disappear because the student dictates the pace of learning in the elective class. The integration of online conferencing within the American life provides the opportunity for teachers to evaluate student products without being in the same physical space. In a post-COVID world, this situation could continue without any real hardship. Performance-based electives that *must* be held on campus (i.e., band ensembles, theatrical plays, agriculture, art, etc.) can be reimagined in a "lab-based" mindset for students to work collaboratively on projects and class work while on campus. Each student would complete the independent learning of the music piece or scene performance outside school periods. They would then come together to practice with the entire band or the drama production during those determined times on campus.

It is the middle time of day that provides the largest amount of risk during a pandemic for the students in a hybrid model. Referencing the daily hybrid schedule model outlined in Figure 10, there is 30 minutes for the students from one class to be isolated into an area of the campus for pick up and the inclusion of the next classes of students for school. A key decision must be the systematic isolation of the ninth and tenth graders to a portion of the school campus for extraction that is free from the inclusive area of the eleventh and twelfth graders. This task is a very large one that must be built for each individual school district and school site.

This schedule is designed for safety during a pandemic but can be utilized for a traditional model. The most noticeable trait for this schedule is the timeframes, which results in the appearance of an extended school day for teachers. This is not true. The linchpin to this system is in the scheduling of classes and the combining of a teacher to a set of students for the year. This ensures that teachers are exposed to students for half the day, with the remainder being utilized for administrative, online, and preparatory work. Properly scheduling the amount of time on campus to match the student population will ensure the safety of everybody involved.

Figure 10 outlines that the ninth and tenth grade teachers would be on campus from approximately 7:30 a.m. until 12:30 p.m. After the appropriate lunch break, the teachers would then be free to leave the campus and complete their school-day preparations in their home settings. These tasks would include the preparation for the next day's lessons, grading, intervention meetings, and collaborative work within their given framework roles.

Conversely, the teachers of 11th- and 12th-grade students would not access the school until 1 p.m. Prior to that timeframe, teachers would be doing the preparation as previously outlined for the 9th- and 10th-grade teachers, which completes the typical, eight-hour day outlined in most contracts. So an 11th- or 12th-grade teacher would actually start their day at approximately 10 a.m. with their preparation and other work, with a portion of that time being travel time to the school site. Given that the end time is 6 p.m. most days, it is not inconceivable for a district to come to an agreement with their teachers on when exactly they should begin their school day. That crucial conversation is district and site specific and should be conducted in this manner.

Extracurricular activities and afterschool programs on the school site can be a concern with regard to the hybrid schedule. Given that 9th- and 10th-grade classes would be a morning-only school experience, it does beg the question as to what those students would do in an afterschool program setting. Interestingly, there should be no change to the application of sports. If coaches who are on campus are matched with the same class sets, their coaching duties could begin away from the campus on the appropriate fields during the outlined times from 1 to 6 p.m. Additionally, contracts for coaches outline that time spent on sports should be outside the regular contracted times. This flexibility of morning or evening practice could foster better coaching by incentivizing coaching at lower levels because they will have more time with their families.

The inverse would occur for the 11th- and 12th-grade sports teams practicing on the campus during the morning schedule of 8:00 – 11:00 a.m. This would put a strain on the necessary club organizations that would be meeting during the school periods. The remedy for this particular situation is the inclusion of other club advisers from different classes. For example, an Interact Club could have an underclassman meeting that could start at 12:30 p.m. and end at 1:30 p.m. with the upper-class meeting happening at 8:00 a.m., during the same time as sports—but in a different portion of the school. Also, excluding the pandemic or other restrictions that limit people on the campus, the lunch period and egress time from 12:00 – 1:00 p.m. could be an opportunity for both sets of classes to intermingle in a club atmosphere.

Ingress and egress of students is an area that is a potential risk on a high school campus. For safety reasons, the number of students must be limited on the campus to the lowest capacities possible to ensure that the number of students commingling is held to a minimum. Given a typical cohort class size of approximately 600 students, it is conceivable to control the meeting and interactivity of 1,200 students versus a complete, campus-wide, 2,400-student-body population. The tactical action plan for both ingress and egress will need to be examined at the school site level because of the architecture and layout of each individual school. Traffic patterns, bus route processes, and street access must be analyzed in order to make the most efficient yet safe walking path for the public.

Some concerns could be raised regarding the late finishing of a school day and the impact of that school day on the different families in a given area. Many stories are shared with imagery of tiny, innocent children being left in cold, dark areas of remote places, leaving them vulnerable to the dark world of society that is around them. These images can happen in isolated incidents but can be completely negligible and eliminated with the proper foresight and planning. What most proponents of this imagery fail to recognize is the fact that most students with excellent grades participate in an afterschool activity and/or sport that far surpasses 6:00 p.m. A majority of the 10th- to 12th-grade students have access to cars and/ or carpooling, which positively impacts the ability of the students to evacuate the school in a safe manner at a later time. Designating certain areas for the 11th-and 12th-graders to congregate after school in a safe manner in order for them to be picked up by appropriate people is a section of the action plan.

Childcare and supervision have been major challenges for families during the COVID-19 experience. Some parents are unable to provide supervision for their students while they are working. This situation has provided some students the opportunity to not be as productive as they generally would under a more specific supervision process. The population of latchkey kids (I was one) would not agree with the situation of students demonstrating their true grit.

A central element of incorporating a hybrid model should be the different resources available to parents for their students to participate in various activities, either on the campus or from their homes. Additionally, parents must be advised to have crucial conversations on topics like setting clear expectations, frequent communication regarding school, and tough conversations with their students, so they can assist with the hybrid model implementation. It is completely understandable that the beginning will be rough, in that a new pattern of lifestyle must be established for families; however, families can develop different opportunities as time continues for their students to thrive in these new schedules.

The hybrid schedule is designed specifically to have the younger students on the campus during the business day that is the norm for most other grades in the educational system, so the flexibility of the family is at a negligible level. Families will drop off their students at the appropriate time (as they have for years). Pick up of their students at the appropriate times allows

for more efficient retrieval of elementary school brothers and sisters. As the years progress and the independence of the student begins to flourish, families could now be more proactive in establishing a career for a student or continued exploration of college enrollment. Opportunities built outside the school environment

could benefit not only the students but also their family finances.
It used to be that older students would be on school campuses for
approximately two to three hours after school, then go on to a job
where they would be able to earn their own money. The result was
an exhausted student going to bed at 11 p.m., with homework still
to be done.

New opportunities can really assist those families in need by
giving their students the ability to get a job that incorporates a
portion of regular business hours. Those students could gain
work in outdoor trades, which are more prevalent during daylight
hours. Collegiate training could then occur during evening hours.
Academically driven students would have more opportunities at
both the freshman and sophomore levels to perhaps attend a college
class in the afternoons. These opportunities could further interests and academic achievements that are independent of the high
school experience. High school can be a gateway to the success of
the student, regardless of their status, family situation, or position.
Every student will have the opportunity to explore whatever path
they (and their family) choose, not one that is based on what educational experts expect of them.

One added benefit could be that elective credit can be expanded
to sources well outside the school offerings. Trade schools and corporate certifications obtained outside the school setting could be
verified by the counseling department to provide elective credit.
This would allow the student who wishes to excel in the mechanical
or construction fields to explore those avenues with tangible results.
Apprenticeships and internships could equally translate into elective credit so the student can gain the necessary experience without
sacrificing school opportunities. Industries could begin training

programs on the latest equipment and techniques at society's pace without the constraints of the educational system, which could generate a labor force at society's informational speed. Corporate trades that require licensing could start their tutelage at a younger age so that graduates would have opportunities of career advancement immediately after graduation. The opportunities of achieving school credit and valuable job experience will give huge benefits to students.

Distance Learning

COVID-19 has dictated the distance learning requirement with all its downfalls and successes. Every school has battled and struggled with this model for the past year. Obvious considerations that must be at the forefront of any new generation of a distance learning process would be the refinement of the online process for student success. It must improve methods of effective interventional support well beyond the current offerings. Once the pandemic dissipates, efforts to continue and expand the online learning process must be as diligent as they were at the beginning of this pandemic era. Accessibility to online capabilities must still be a major goal of every school district in this nation so that all students can have access to the opportunities available to them. Continued improvements of online platforms must also progress for a more seamless integration and sharing of information. However, the most important work that needs to continue after this pandemic must be the continued improvements of virtual meetings and the abilities for students and teachers to share a classroom setting in a virtual experience. At the top of that work must be increased abilities for sharing and collaboration with students and teachers.

The elimination of ground noise could make it a seamless process. In a traditional setting, teachers would be able to hold a five-second private conversation with someone at a whisper level. They might be reclarifying a particular word for a student who might be struggling with the English language. They might be correcting behavior processes or keeping students on task. They might be giving them that most important, positive reinforcement that the student is doing a great job. Regardless of the message, the ability for a teacher to have the smallest private conversation for building trusting relationships is a critical element of the classroom.

Another area of improvement must be in the monitoring of student interaction with the ability to give instantaneous feedback based on attention. Teachers have a very hard time keeping students on task and are unsure if the student is putting the educational class as a background while doing other things. Some of the multitaskers in this new generation do not have the prioritization skills and focus to complete their tasks through self-motivation, which ultimately has a negative effect. In the traditional setting, the teacher would step into a classroom and provide the support necessary for students to grow in this area of life skills. However, the virtual environment is very limited in its ability to support that exchange. Establishing a private, non-face-to-face, instantaneous feedback process would allow teachers the ability to monitor students while doing presentation processes which would mimic the experience of a school classroom.

All in all, the educational family should celebrate how wonderfully they have been able to adapt to this particular pandemic. If there is ever an innovative process that has been started, it has been in the area of education. This petri dish of exploration has truly become a model where private enterprise (Google, Blackboard and Canvas), has been able to work collaboratively with educational institutions and state-run organizations in order to provide contents to students in a safe manner. We, the educators of the world, have maintained our fiduciary duty of educating our students under extraordinary circumstances. There are areas to improve, but the core spirit of the educator stands vigilant to the purpose.

Chapter 11

Teacher Roles

The restructuring of the teaching profession is no small matter. Institutional systems took decades to refine and solidify into the process that exists today. However, all the different programs, school designs, management processes, and structures stem from the same picture of education—the one-room schoolhouse. With some exceptions, the picture of a singular teacher overseeing student progress is the cornerstone upon which all programs are built.

The restructuring of education demands a different cornerstone that will include all the societal advances that complicate teaching. This new cornerstone must be the student, for they are the product that is created by this system. I know there have been numerous initiatives and mission statements that claim to be centered on student learning, but these devolve quickly into teacher-centered plans; that is, teachers create all the learning processes.

This is a drastic change from the plausible deniability of most districts because the plan is specialized to the community it serves. For far too long, districts have taken the easy way out by adopting the "one size fits all" programs from publishers who are supposed experts in education. The programs promote a labyrinth of resources available to teachers, so *they* can create the plan for each student. These resources, although constructive, are rarely implemented because of the most important factor—time. Teachers spend hours trying to learn new technologies, access procedures, and develop plans. *Maintaining* those plans for 200 students is an impossibility. So when districts throw this at teachers, few should wonder why there is little response.

This new framework of teacher roles establishes an environment that provides enough time and resources for the teachers to create the highest quality of education for their students, with feedback prior to presentation of the content. The old method of adjusting plans after initial implementation will change to the creation of the best quality at the beginning. An added benefit is the leveraging of quality teaching across disciplines. Some of the most engaging teachers who present content with great results are not qualified to offer the content because they are not "highly qualified" at the start. This new framework could allow the PE coach, who is the best interventionist with students, to influence math classes without losing the quality of the subject matter.

So subsequent teaching roles are reimagined with the sole purpose of segmenting sections for teachers to exhibit or develop expertise. Other aspects of society have ventured in similar changes with extraordinary results. From the assembly line to Google team-oriented work groups, the idea of incorporating numerous talents toward a singular goal has generated success. The challenge of change is monumental and must be based in some part on the current system. In order to gain a collective commitment from teachers unions and management, there needs to be a direct link to the current system. So the new responsibilities will be created from a current structure—the California Standard of the Teaching Profession (CSTP). The roles are offered to transform teaching for true student success. The conceptualization of this program is summarized in Figure 11.

Figure 11: New Teacher Roles

Presenter	Facilitator	Interventionist	Developer
Presenter / Delivery Standard 1	Social Emotional / Diversity Standard 2	Intervening Strategies & Extensions Standard 3	Curriculum Specialist / Assessment Standard 4 & 5
Presentations	Teaming	Grading	Learning Objectives
Checking for Understanding	School Culture integration (MTSS)	Extension opportunities	Alignment with standards
Formative assessment	EL strategies	SPED Interventions	Pacing
Grading	Grading	Grading	Grading

Each role is further explained in the following sections. The key overview the reader needs to take is that this is a group of specialists who continually convene for individual student achievement. Because the responsibilities are so focused, the teacher is free to create comprehensive plans and supports for the development of the student.

Presenter/Delivery

STANDARD ONE:

Engaging and supporting all students in learning

   1.1 Using knowledge of students to engage them in learning

   1.2 Connecting learning to students' prior knowledge, backgrounds, life experiences, and interests

   1.3 Connecting subject matter to meaningful, real-life contexts

   1.4 Using a variety of instructional strategies, resources, and technologies to meet students' diverse learning

   1.5 Promoting critical thinking through inquiry, problem solving, and reflection

   1.6 Monitoring student learning and adjusting instruction while teaching

   1.7 Using instructional time to optimize learning

The position of the presenter is the face of the subject matter because they are the most seen by the students. The presenter is truly subject competent and focuses on the instruction of the teaching. Their directive is to convey the clearest messages of the curriculum to the students. Incorporation of new instructional strategies and technology will be their research focus when not directly in front of students. Reflection on all aspects of the above standards will be their daily focus. Technology companies who strive to make the classroom more efficient have teams of people generating a single interactive aspect of student feedback (i.e. a survey). Yet the expectation is for the teacher to effectively integrate that student feedback tool within the class. They must also train themselves and students to master it within a minute. Specializing this portion of teaching will provide the evaluation of effective integration the students deserve.

This teacher must explore and implement the most effective interactive tools for the classroom presentation. All these dimensions in the presentation phase have been reimagined by technology at a mind-boggling rate. For the best instruction to occur, energy needs to be spent, maximizing these tools at the speed of technology while maintaining the consistency for all students. Inclusion of different styles of engagement tools is the key directive for this position. For example, effective use of music can be used to reinforce the theme of a presentation, using graphics that provide the most engagement without overloading the students' eyes, and sequencing the lesson for the best strategic placement of checking for understanding.

Another key challenge is ensuring that students can access the class information despite the problems that occur from access. Environmental challenges demand that class concepts be flexible in their presentation. One key responsibility for the presenter position is the filming of support videos for students. Small vignettes that clarify each aspect of the overall lessons should be generated for each student to access on their own schedule. Example films can be generated to promote critical thinking within the student. Extension education opportunities should be offered for students to branch out and gain knowledge in other disciplines or go deeper into a subject at a higher level.

One reason why teachers enter the profession is the spark that is generated when a student is awakened to a new world through a particular concept. There is always one genre of literature that students find intriguing and want to know more. A key age in history that a student finds more fascinating and wants to research what life was like in that age. The mathematical concept the student used with a parent in real life that increases their familial relationship through math. All these situations, the fun of teaching, can be achieved once again by providing these opportunities digitally.

Facilitator /Engagement – Social Emotional -Diversity
STANDARD TWO:

2.1 Promoting social development and responsibility within a caring community where each student is treated fairly and respectfully

2.2 Creating physical or virtual learning environments that promote student learning, reflect diversity, and encourage constructive and productive interactions among students

2.3 Establishing and maintaining learning environments that are physically, intellectually, and emotionally safe

2.4 Creating a rigorous learning environment with high expectations and appropriate support for all students

2.5 Developing, communicating, and maintaining high standards for individual and group behavior

2.6 Employing classroom routines, procedures, norms, and supports for positive behavior to ensure a climate in which all students can learn

The creativity and individuality of assessment is a challenge that most teachers struggle with on a daily basis. The time necessary to create assessments that truly incorporate special education (SPED) and english language literacy (ELL) accommodations does not exist in the timeframe of a regular school year. This position looks at all portions of the educational journey through the lens of understanding the materials and skills. This engagement person will implement checking for understanding and monitor their success. Integration of EL strategies will advance language acquisition at a higher rate than the current system. The addition of the adjusted assessments will allow teachers to verify knowledge and skills required by their respective state laws.

Many teachers have the talents to engage students in different, group-style activities. One key aspect of learning is the kinesthetic use of knowledge in a team-oriented process. Teachers do amazing things, from scavenger hunts to puzzle creation to multi-tiered obstacle courses, in dealing with the concept. The genres of literature circles and writing circles encapsulate the necessity of teamwork, along with the proving of a particular concept. Advanced organizations like Advancement Via Individual Determination (AVID) have structured activities for students to learn to communicate and conceptualize learning in real-life situations. The purpose of these engagements is to increase teamwork, prove knowledge, and build a dialectical base for students to improve themselves. The facilitator would create these multifaceted engagements for strategic utilization within the classroom. In consultation with the rest of the team, they would identify specific places within the curricular structure to implement these lessons in order for students to experience these types of processes. A key attribute of this position is the ability for this teacher to look holistically at the engagement, purpose, outcome, and reflection of each group activity for a better student experience.

Additionally, this position will evaluate the level of diversity within the curriculum. Once again, time limits the ability for curriculum adjustment under the current structure. Adaptation of assessments and presentations to include EL strategies or support will be a requirement. Research must be conducted to find resources for ESL students to understand concepts in both English and their native languages. Different assessments will be created to reflect content and not language acquisition. Feedback to students will be a major focus for this person. The facilitator will consistently evaluate the responses of students and their needs. From this feedback, the teacher will generate different extension strategies for language acquisition while evaluating the procedures and assessments to the rest of the students. They must reconcile different strategies and types of assessments to match the student's response capabilities. Remember, the ultimate goal of assessment is proving the adaptation of skill through the acquisition of standards. This new position can ensure mastery of skills for some of the most vulnerable populations.

One area that is a challenge for most schools is the participation of teachers and their perspectives within committees on the campus. Year after year, requests go out for teachers to participate in English Learner Advisory Committee (ELAC) or African American Parent Advisory Council (AAPAC), only to be met with silence. This response is not laziness upon the teacher's part but rather focus on the learning for the students, which limits their abilities to be a part of that process. The facilitator would have a mandated requirement to participate within those diversity committees so the classroom perspective is communicated to the community. Decision making can include aspects and behaviors within the classroom for better student achievement. Listening to parents and community members regarding the effects of the classroom on diverse students can then be interpreted and restructured for implementation within the curriculum process in a consistent manner. Finally, the communication loop between the community and the classroom can grow evermore close.

In addressing the social/emotional aspects of the student experience, this teacher would monitor and assist in creating formative processes for augmentation of student behavior to a norm that would increase the classroom environment. In consultation with the administration, the facilitator could conduct referrals for alternative behavior programs. These programs guide reflective practices similar to the alternative-to-suspension program and restoration conferences. By providing the opportunity for students to learn behavioral strategies of reconciliation and exchange in a more targeted method, students will be able to more quickly gain, in real time, the necessary tools for working with others.

The final area of focus for this role is the integration of school culture within the learning experience of students. Many initiatives have been implemented to modify student behavior to positively contribute to schools. Current programs such as Multi-Tiered System of Support (MTSS), Building Assets, Reducing Risks Program (BARR), and Positive Behavior Interventions and Supports (PBIS) seek to establish a structured educational experience of positive decision making and behavior for students to positively coexist on campus. Additionally, the school binds students together in a common culture for the betterment of the school's identity. The current challenge has been to incorporate these additional foci into an already overwhelmed system. Most implementation plans treat this additional learning as a separate curriculum that is inserted into the calendar. The tradition is to stop the regular learning process for this "thing we have to teach" and then go back to the regularly scheduled programming. This implementation method creates easy forms of denial or "a waste of time" by students and staff.

The facilitator can match the school culture lessons into the curriculum so that both are taught simultaneously. Benefits of this system would be a verifiable inclusion of school culture and identity without losing precious minutes. These targets can be manifested in assessment examples, class activities, renovated assignments, etc. that could reinforce the school identity through the curriculum. These situations do not have to be the case. The facilitator, along with the presenter, can focus on including these necessary discussion topics within their respective curriculums in order to influence school culture. Choosing discussion questions for English classes that discuss violence in all its forms can be given within stories that are read. Mathematics could graph the feelings of student surveys on school climate. These examples are the smallest ideas that could be generated by teaching professionals to provide the most comprehensive learning experiences.

Interventionist/Strategies & Extensions
STANDARD THREE:

3.1. Demonstrating knowledge of subject matter, academic content standards, and curriculum frameworks

3.2. Applying knowledge of student development and proficiencies to ensure student understanding of subject matter

3.3. Organizing curriculum to facilitate student understanding of the subject matter

3.4. Utilizing instructional strategies that are appropriate to the subject matter

3.5. Using and adapting resources, technologies, and standards-aligned instructional materials, including adopted materials, to make subject matter accessible to all students

3.6. Addressing the needs of English learners and students with special needs to provide equitable access to the content

Time after time it is stated that special education teachers are the most undervalued and overused teachers within any school culture. These individuals are masters at taking complex situations and meeting students at their academic levels. They assist students with functioning inside the classroom, further explaining the curriculum, and motivating them for success. From helping to organize their planners to chunking their education in smaller sizes so that students can prove mastery, these teachers really have a unique situation for each struggling student. These experts must investigate the key issue that limits the learning and innovative methods for the success of each unique student. The challenge has always been that this particular teacher needs to extract a student from the regular educational environment in order to create a focused situation for that success to occur. This is done in the hope that eventually the student can be re-introduced into the educational environment with the necessary tools for them to be successful or maintain success in the regular educational environment.

By specializing this particular person across the entire student population, their talents could be widespread across a number of different classrooms throughout the entire school. They can create different forms of curriculum and intervention videos that could speak to a number of different students. This teacher would generate interventional supports (e.g., graphic organizers, step-by step instructions, etc.) within the regular curriculum presentation.

Additionally, they would produce structured review lessons that are palatable to those struggling in a particular area. In collaboration with the team, these teachers can generate different graphic organizing tools that assist students in creating complex assignments. Conferencing can be maximized with smaller groups of students who might be struggling. The stigma of special education or English language acquisition will be minimized because the interventionalist teachers work with students who are struggling with a concept, regardless of category. The student's experience is made easier by another teacher helping out all students.

One of the most valuable elements of separating and specializing these teachers is the ability for the interventionalist to look across the curriculum of the entire learning process and provide necessary input for assessments. Feedback on assessment questions for different modalities can be generated by this person. The interventionalist can collaborate with the rest of the team to generate "support videos" for all students to succeed. These podcast videos created from an array of screencast software, made popular throughout the pandemic, can offer subjects like comma usage, paper formats, calculation models, and other segments of learning. For those students with IEPs, behavioral observations, and knowledge of class work can be organically collected and analyzed in a consistent manner with increased points of interaction between the students and support. One of the most important things the interventionalist can provide is the feeling to every student that they are not alone and there is no shame in not being the absolute best in everything. Good teaching is good teaching, regardless of the level of the student. Although the focus of every aspect of teaching must be to the benefit of the student, the inclusion of many different techniques to support students who struggle in a specific area is not new and should continue to be developed.

To be clear, this role is not solely for special education professionals. Extensions and advanced challenges are also created for students who excel in certain concepts. The brainstorming of extended readings or learning opportunities for students to delve deeper into skills they excel at are generated by the interventionalist. Career-related pathways of concepts are generated for students to investigate further avenues for success. The purpose behind this is to guide students to explore different opportunities they might not have thought of previously, based on skills those students excel at. There is no limit to the effect these resources might add to the prospects for students.

Developer / Curriculum & Assessment
STANDARD FOUR:

4.1. Using knowledge of students' academic readiness, language proficiency, cultural background, and individual development to plan instruction

4.2. Establishing and articulating goals for student learning

4.3. Developing and sequencing long-term and short-term instructional plans to support student learning

4.4. Planning instruction that incorporates appropriate strategies to meet the learning needs of all students

4.5. Adapting instructional plans and curricular materials to meet the assessed learning needs of all students

STANDARD FIVE:

5.1. Applying knowledge of the purposes, characteristics, and uses of different types of assessments

5.2. Collecting and analyzing assessment data from a variety of sources to inform instruction

5.3. Reviewing data, both individually and with colleagues, to monitor student learning

5.4. Using assessment data to establish learning goals and to plan, differentiate, and modify instruction

5.5. Involving all students in self-assessment, goal setting, and monitoring progress

5.6. Using available technologies to assist in assessment, analysis, and communication of student learning

5.7. Using assessment information to share timely and comprehensible feedback with students and their families

Many teachers continue their education after joining the ranks of the teaching corps. They seek further validation and knowledge in the field to improve some facet of the teaching style. Some specialize in the leadership aspect and gain an overall view of the learning process and how to facilitate these methods in leadership roles. Others specialize in the more granular instruction models. It is these individuals who become experts in curriculum development, outcome generation, and a comprehensive learning experience.

The developer position is created for the purpose of providing these experts the opportunity to directly impact the teaching of the entire department. Because there are multiple developers within a discipline, more people have the opportunity to directly use their talents. The first reaction would be to have a singular person in this role; however, this position could have additional teachers. The decision would be predicated on the situation of the department and their current use of technology. These individuals view the craft of teaching from a three-mile-high perspective. During most meetings, the Developer is the facilitator. They are the collector of the contributions from the other team members, who then build the comprehensive teaching model for the team. Teaching logistics is done by this role through the maintenance of the collective educational platform and the development of learning within it.

These individuals create the concrete plan and calendar the course for the entire year. As the standards outline, the developer forms the overall plan of instruction. It is their central role to develop and articulate the goals for student learning. Central to every aspect of this position is the ability to listen to all stakeholders—fellow teachers, students, administrators, and parents—and gather collective commitments from the other team members. They become the clearinghouse of information from the other team members and research the resources necessary for success. As the team continues to create and contribute from their respective positions and perspectives, this individual keeps the central focus of long-term goals in mind and evaluates the implementation of ideas through the lens of those long-term and short-term goals.

Their central feedback mechanism is to consistently interview students to know that the student can articulate the "why" of the lesson and the knowledge the student intends to get from the class. Observation of student achievement through results of assessments, both formative and summative, along with direct observations, will provide this individual with a necessary landscape of student achievements. Results are then communicated back to the body of teachers within the team so that adjustments, additions, and changes to the learning process can take place in a seamless manner.

The developer would focus their constructive time in forming and analyzing all student data. They would verify alignment of all assessments to the focused standards for students' achievements. Additionally, they would sequence the many types of questions that provide multiple opportunities for students to repeatedly attempt mastery. Another challenge most teachers have is the variable situations that occur with access to students. Whether access is limited by illness, suspension, school activities, or family vacations, there are times when assessments are eliminated from student grades because the student is not able to take the assessment at the appropriate time. Teachers stop the assessment process for fear of student cheating and/or answers being given out between the time the student returns and the assessment process, which skews the actual assessment. Another contributing factor is that the student's return is so far down the calendar of the class that it is counter-productive to provide the assessment without overwhelming the student. One particular duty of this position would be to draft and create multiple opportunities for students to be assessed that are free from timeframes. By shifting the assessment to a true skills-based process, students can be assessed regardless of whatever timeframe is given. It will be the task of the Curriculum/Assessment person to create and maintain the necessary blocks of questions that can be utilized to assess students.

The developer also becomes a direct conduit to the site- and district-level administrators. Monitoring conversations districtwide can be conducted with accurate measurements and direct observation without inhibiting the learning experience. Internal and external monitoring scans can be conducted districtwide by this individual, who then reports back to district personnel. These conclusions can then contribute to outcomes necessary for appropriate funding and resource allocation. Evaluation of developer interviews by district personnel throughout the entire district could provide a more in-depth conversation, with the direct result being a more comprehensive understanding for decision making. Personnel will comprehensively evaluate the acceptance of textbooks, outside resources, and technology.

As the person responsible for extension lessons, the developer will generate the unit blocks necessary to include new types of literature or concepts for the learning experience. Student interest surveys can play a key role in the nuanced development of lessons within a curriculum. Career application lessons can be conceptualized for students to bridge education with real-life career aspirations. These opportunities will generate interest in a multitude of career pathways by students.

Districts force new curriculums into the classroom throughout a school year. The developer can focus their efforts on the different possibilities for students to show their mastery of concepts through their own interests. The choosing of diverse resources and readings could generate a multitude of mastery opportunities for students. One example is in English Language Arts. Newer literature integration to foster student, self-driven exploration rarely happens. Genres of literature are not explored because of time. The "approved" classics are used again and again because teachers already have the assessments completed, and they do not want to constantly regenerate all aspects of the classroom.

Another example would be in the subject of history. Currently, the U.S. Constitution is regurgitated based on a single adult perspective. The methods of showing mastery could change significantly. In the future, a student from another country could compare the U.S. Constitution to their country of origin's constitution and describe why it is better to live in the United States. Student-generated films, slideshows, drawings, writings, or even TikTok dances could be used as assessments of a new concept. All these explorations are just the tip of the iceberg for the developer, keeping in mind that their motto is to explore how students demonstrate mastery.

This is not to say that contributions from other team members should not be welcome. Teachers continually come up with assessment methods while generating other components of the learning experience. The developer would welcome these new contributions and align them to the collective experience of the student. Interestingly, the required need for further collaboration of appropriate test questions could foster further advice, sharing, and other methods of teachers to improve their own practices. For example, the presenter could share some options for questions to be given based on the presentations provided to students. During the sharing, feedback could be given by the developer to the presenter in methods and ways that the presenter might not be aligned with the curriculum. Additionally, there are opportunities for reinforced support and praise during these exchanges between the teachers, which then results in increased trust. The new innovation system will start this transformational change to a more flexible and student-centered learning environment.

Chapter 12

Other Areas to Consider

Master Schedule Assignments

The master schedule is the quintessential strategic plan for any school site. The culture and focus of any site are present in the offerings of the school. Some people have said that the schedule is the best tool to influence any school culture and outline the priorities for its students. The typical high school master schedule board is organized by subject matter and teacher because the law requires that teachers must be credentialed to teach these certain courses. The changes outlined in this book provide an additional need to innovate the structure of this process to mirror the new framework. The key to a good schedule has always been balance across the offerings, and this directive will not change. The main change will be to create a further segmentation of the schedule that includes teaming teachers to create the outline for the additional roles in the framework.

The organization of the master schedule based on the new framework is configured by subject and teacher. The difference is the addition of the role the teacher will play in the subject offering. The organizer must ensure the balance of the roles in addition to the subject preparations. As a reminder, these course framework changes are meant only for the core classes, with electives staying to the traditional method. Most teacher contracts restrict a teacher from being assigned to three or more preparations during a school year. This requirement can become more flexible, given that the demands of the teachers will be smaller and more focused. So discussions of teachers being assigned to four or five different subject matters can be conducted, with certain limitations. It would not be overwhelming for a teacher to be the assessment specialist for all four English subjects. There should be a word of caution in mainstreaming an isolated method such as this because this pattern would need the necessary collaboration for the best results. Team-oriented processes must be balanced as well. An example of a master schedule is presented in Figure 12.

Figure 12: Master Schedule Example

Teacher Name	Period 1	Period 2	Period 3	Period 4	Period 5	Period 6
Teacher 1	Eng 2 Developer (Primary)	Eng 1 Facilitator (Secondary)	Eng 2 Developer (Primary)	Eng 2 Developer (Primary)	Eng 1 Facilitator (Secondary)	Elective

Many teachers have a core class assignment and an elective offering as well. These situations must be dealt with carefully so as to not overwhelm the teacher. Crucial conversations must be held with these individuals regarding upcoming assignments and their goals as a teacher. Educational leaders always strive to continue teacher development, and these conversations will be necessary to foster these plans.

As always, the final decisions must be focused on fulfilling the prime directive of the school and not the interests of the teachers. The demands of the core class offerings must be completed first, with electives being filled in after the core schedule is complete. This procedure contradicts the traditional creation of the master schedule with placing the single-offering class first and growing from there. The prime directive is given the priority it deserves.

Some natural feedback to this is the concern that the school will not offer many electives (if any) with this new model. Remember, the elective credit can be given from other institutions or verified organizations. This demand requires the district to maintain a large referral list of recommended offerings outside the school setting. Focusing teachers on their fiduciary responsibility will provide the highest quality education.

Staff Assignments for Student Movement

High school educators are traditionally assigned a room, and students rotate through this room over the course of a day. In the new framework, the teacher would roam, similar to a college process. The rooms will be assigned based on the space the necessary tasks need. Buildings could be assigned by grade level, which would assist in a possible hybrid model. Larger spaces can be utilized for class-wide input and guest speakers. For example, theaters and gyms could be used to introduce access to new apps or initiatives. Additionally, assessments can be conducted using these spaces.

The key premise is that the teacher teams create a plan for each term and offer that plan to the administrator for final assignment at the beginning of the term. Intervention rooms would be designated for teacher teams to interact with students for continued learning. These intervention rooms would be assigned by the teacher teams for the best intervention. Rooms for extension lessons could be established for a similar purpose. Admittedly, this process seems chaotic because teachers are used to having their own "space" to feel comfortable teaching. It is here that teachers find their role. Each role is not determined by the space but by the materials needed to complete the job.

Buildings need to be assigned that provide the best success for the given spaces. Some schools are constructed with buildings with an interior core or "pod." This type of configuration might really work with subject matters being the first consideration and grade level being the next. Other configurations with large buildings might use the inverse to separate the campus by grade first and then by subject. This decision will have to be a site decision that is collaborative with the instructors. But again, a word of caution to not return to the same thing as before. Students must travel to where they can get the most gain and not where the teachers think they themselves might be the most comfortable.

Finally, school schedules must be included in the decision making. Whatever configuration is decided, it must be run through each possible schedule in order to maintain the flexibility of the future. A cross check must be conducted with the thoughts of a traditional day, a hybrid day, a small cohort day and a virtual day. Finalizing this plan provides the flexibility of the school to react to the societal needs with minimal chaos.

Discipline Changes

The old saying that the cogs of justice grind slowly is still true. The pandemic has highlighted areas of education code that were lacking in the areas of discipline. The virtual environment has established the need to re-evaluate discipline regulation like California Education Code Section 48900. Violations of class norms in a virtual classroom are not outlined for use by administrators. This places the burden on assistant principals, who are forced to interpret the traditional rules and apply them to this new situation. These extrapolations place the administrators—and the district—in legal jeopardy because the rules are open to interpretation. Additional rule violations need to be created for the virtual environment, with the appropriate behavior modification and structured discipline plan.

Adding to the confusion is the methods of discipline. In traditional settings, common wisdom was that the student needed to be exiled from the school site when the safety of self or others was in jeopardy. Suspension was the remedy chosen in order to separate the student for a time of reflection and familial influence. This remedy does not apply to a virtual situation when the student is already at home. Some student behaviors have been magnified in order to pit the school against the parent, with the student's goal being to avoid participation in school in order to gain more free time. Students augment the contact information of parents—especially, parents with language barriers—so that all school communication comes to them. There are a myriad of other behaviors that limit the influence the school can have on student behavior.

Many programs have been created to guide student behavior through conferences, reflection, and restoration. It is in this realm that the innovation can positively affect student behavior and maintain the classroom. Once a student violates a rule, the student would still be separated from the class until they complete a learning journey. Virtual modules with assignments can be created to lead students through appropriate behavior modifications. The advancement of this process will need to be the inclusion of parents within the process. Parents must review specific portions of the behavioral program. Admittedly, this does put further pressure on parents during a stressful time, and it does not seem fair. The response is that the school is not ultimately responsible for the growth and training of the student—it is the parent's responsibility.

Most teachers see a student for 180 hours over the course of a single year. The expectation that teachers are to modify years of behavior through trust in this small amount of time is unrealistic. Most teachers have examples where they have accomplished this very thing, but these are rare and special. The parent holds the moral responsibility of molding their child's behavior to acceptable levels within society. It is for this reason that the parent needs to be an active part of the process. If the parent fails to assist, then referrals and follow up with school counselors and therapists could be engaged to support the parent through the process.

Parent Training and Roll-Out

The current norm for a parent in a high school is a passive/aggressive relationship. Parents entrust their children to the school with the belief the school will do what is good for the student, which will make their child happy. The monumental benefit of this situation is that parents do not have to worry about a major aspect of their child's development. We have seen this based on the increased responsibilities slowly being assumed by the school. Schools have taken on behavioral development, food assistance, mental and physical health, entertainment, pride, and even babysitting. Although all of these services are rightly offered at the school site because it is a population hub of the community, the responsibility of making them effective has also been transferred by the parent. Parents are generally missing during the creation and implementation process of these services.

There are a number of justifiable reasons for this situation. Both parents generally work during business hours. Parent relationships with the school are based on their own experiences and produce distrust in the process. Language barriers and societal perceptions cause parents to hide because of feeling inferior or are perhaps undocumented residents. As long as the child does not complain and seems happy, then all is well. Additionally, if the services are not offered to the satisfaction of the parents, they can then blame the school and ensure plausible deniability. To be clear, parents are not to blame for this situation, but their participation in the process should be recognized when the criticism comes to the forefront of "ruining my child's life."

In order for this new school plan to be truly successful, clarity of message must be a high priority for districts that adopt the framework. The use of social media and other district platforms across all stakeholders does not need to be explored in order to state that it is the paramount method of reaching and communicating to all stakeholders in a school community. These methods might need to be expanded or leveraged, but there must be a clear focus on these efforts. To that end, instructional videos that singularly outline new school changes must be generated by the school district, with the implementation of the framework in small bites. It is a crucial component to establish the foundation of understanding prior to implementation of the new framework.

Some communities do not have a comprehensive online process for successful messaging. For these populations, the new framework procedures must be given in writing and in person in order for the stakeholders to really understand the changes. The promotion needs to be offered through news media organizations in online, print, and video media. News media can be leveraged, along with social media, so that feedback can be exchanged, and understanding can be built. Explicit conversations in the reasoning for these changes and opportunities for feedback must also be conducted prior to final implementation so that the community is included in the process. Local businesses must be alerted to the new opportunities for a new labor force. Local committee organizations and advocacy groups must also be included at the very beginning of this promotional campaign in order for them to be able to not only agree with and support the program but also advocate for the program in their meetings with their supporters. Key advocate parents must also be included in the beginning stages of the process so they can promote among the different social aspects of the community. By building the collective commitment of the key stakeholders within any community, the program will be as clear as possible, with the community adopting the new measures because they will have been provided feedback and will understand the intent of the framework. Implementation of this framework is a 9- to 12-week process so that all stakeholders will understand on day one the requirements and benefits of the new program.

These community organizations and key stakeholders will also need to play a role in the initial evaluation process of the program's implementation. They should be given the power to conduct surveys and evaluation measures—on and off campus—to assist in adjusting the framework as needed for the betterment of students. Implicit within this process is the understanding that the district is committing to this process for a 4-year timeframe to prevent knee-jerk reactions of going back to what was once safe.

Chapter 13

Transformational Leaders Needed

The linchpin to this whole process is the need for transformational leadership to be the guiding principle of management during this change. Transformational leaders are significantly more than managers of an organization. These inspirational and innovative effectors of change influence the way people think and behave in work and often in life. They inspire us to challenge our views and help us see new possibilities. These leaders produce an environment where people feel dedicated and committed to achieving a shared vision. They encourage open dialogue and focus on consistent improvement. Our team identified five essential characteristics of an effective leader: they are passionate visionaries, ethical surveyors, inspirational team builders, courageous guiding figures, and charismatic communicators.

A transformational leader is a passionate and charismatic communicator who courageously guides an organization toward an inspired vision. They consistently survey the integrity of the organization to locate areas of strength and refinement while consistently fostering a unified approach toward solutions, all within an ethical framework.

Transformational leaders understand that the goal is to move beyond present-day conditions toward the betterment of the organization and, ultimately, to improve lives. It is the talent of thinking through current situations that has increased civilization throughout history (Burns, 2003, p. 18).

The ambition of transformational leaders is often seen as lofty and out of touch by most standards, but their guidance leads them through the fear toward the desired objective. The initial reaction to these intentions can often include disbelief, ridicule, or rejection. What distinguishes the transformational leader is their ability to frame a concept so that all participants are personally vested in the achievement of the goal. It brings to completion a previously unrealized need for everyone, not just the leader (Howell & Avolio, 1992). The result of these efforts is a complete change of mindset and the establishment of a shared vision, which eventually leads to success (Northouse, 2010, p. 198). Moreover, the transformation trendsetter keeps the established goal at the forefront of all movement within the organization. The desired result is rarely just about a tangible objective. As suggested in the video by Simon Sinek (2009), the transformation power comes from the paradigm shift in participant's thinking rather than the attainment of a particular goal. Leadership is not only a descriptive term but a prescriptive one, embracing a moral, even a passionate, dimension (Burns, 2003).

True movements for improvement are led by those who are motivated by an intrinsic justification. They see a larger, more universal intention, or "why" these changes need to occur. This intention becomes generative, and the internal merit motivates others to join the cause. The leader monitors the movement of the organization through the lens of the moral imperative. Defining a moral imperative, or code of ethics, is daunting. There are many different definitions, and the differences can be significant. Solomon and Hanson provide one definition:

Ethics is, first of all, the quest for, and the understanding of, the good life, of living well a life worth living. It is largely a matter of perspective: proofing every activity and goal in its place, knowing what is worth doing and what is not worth doing, knowing what is worth wanting and having and knowing what is not worth wanting and having (Solomon & Hanson, 1983).

Transformational leaders implement ethical systems to guide the progress of an organization. It is the cooperative set of ground rules used for making what is considered "right" decisions for the organization and the compass for all problem solving and decisions.

Dramatic change in any organization involves creative problem solving. This is supported by Mumford, Zaccaro, Harding et al. "Problem-solving skills are a leader's creative ability to solve new and unusual, ill-defined organizational problems" (2000). For success of the vision, both human and tangible capital must be leveraged in creative yet ethical ways. Genuine relationships become the key to maximizing the full potential of the organization. Northouse suggests ". . . assessing followers' motives, satisfying their needs, and treating them as full human beings" (2010). Tapping into individual strengths can reduce stress among the team and provide effective outcomes (Bass & Riggio, 2006, p. 55). Ethical decisions and authentic relationships increase credibility for the team. It opens the door to transparent conversations about possible pitfalls and helps the team stay true to the goal.

The individual component of transformational leadership emphasizes the necessity of altruism for leadership to be anything more than authoritarian control (Kanungo & Mendonca, 1996, p. 85). The contributions of each member of a transformative organization should be valued and respected. Bass argues that followers who identify with their leaders have high levels of efficiency and productivity (Bass & Riggio, 2006, p. 52). The transformational leader perpetually evaluates the commitment of the team to the task, and any conflict along the way is swiftly mediated. Gaps and goals are identified for each member of the team, while new mindsets are encouraged (Northouse, 2010, p. 186). These processes are accomplished with an unyielding level of integrity. In both work and deed, the transformational leader models the vision and holds everyone, including themselves, accountable for the results (Northouse, 2010, p. 191). This process remains transparent among the whole operation so the team can grow as a cohesive unit as they seek the end goal.

High emotional intelligence and coaching strategies are advantageous for the transformational leader to develop the group and long- and short-term goals (Leban & Zulauf, 2004). These daring individuals are collaborative in nature and humble in announcement (Bass & Riggio, 2006, p. 218). Although they might be charismatic, transformational leaders speak to the achievements of the group and not their role in those accolades. These leaders provide guiding principles for the collective group to immerse themselves in and work towards (Northouse, 2010, p. 197). These individuals accept failure along the way and truly embody a growth mindset (Dweck, 2006) so solutions may be generated and implemented for further refinement. These leaders have keen discernment and help the team stay accountable to the journey. Yet, if paths were to separate, the transformational leader supports all members in their growth as people (Northouse, 2010, p. 191).

It requires mental and moral strength to make bold decisions even when there are dissenters, to say what needs to be said, and to place trust in those they lead. A systematic gathering of feedback is established. The responses influence the procedures and help to monitor the perceptions of the group. Continuous transparency and reflection point out opportunities for change or provide confirmation of the process.

Transformational leaders are masterful communicators across a spectrum of audiences. People walk away from an interaction with these individuals, thinking they were the only concern for the leader. They are active listeners who identify with the circumstances being brought forth, and empathy is consistently communicated. Their words comfort people and make them feel valued. Open-ended questions are implemented to foster differing ideas and perspectives for their audiences. They generate self-reflection and deep thought among listeners while empowering them to strive for future successes. Burns states that values are "power resources for a leadership that would transform society for the fuller realization of the highest moral purposes" (Burns, 2003, p. 213). To promote greater feelings of psychological empowerment, a clear vision should be articulated to inspire employees to take greater responsibility for their work at all organizational levels (Bruce J. Avolio, Weichun Zhu, William Koh, & Puja Bhatia, 2004, p. 963). Understanding employee needs, creating a supportive atmosphere, and engaging in mentoring practices would also likely contribute to a greater feeling of psychological empowerment (Bruce J. Avolio et al., 2004, p. 954).

Transformational leadership skills are paramount for impacting change in a 21st century organization. Simon Sinek, in his book *Start With Why*, shared the critical importance of communicating the values and ideals guiding the actions of a contemporary organization (Sinek, 2011, p. 52). If the values of the organization and the roles of each participant are clearly defined, members are more apt to have internal motivation. There is inherent satisfaction in spending the day working toward your own desired outcomes. We all find great worth in serving a cause we personally believe in.

So let us all become the transformational leaders we are required to become for the future of our civilization. Let us remain centered on our prime directives and create a learning world that provides all students the opportunity to advance themselves. Most of all, let the new age of learning be one that does not calcify again into an immovable structure but one that is flexible enough for future, life-altering realities. Finally, let the school be a school and nothing more.

Let the innovation begin!

Conclusion

T he struggles for every teacher have been real for a very long time. Each day every teacher struggles to balance the multitude of aspects in learning while trying to be flexible in dealing with the increased speed of change required for education. Society's change from a knowledge-based system to an information-based system is making the current position of a classroom teacher in high school almost obsolete. Families and students are starting to not see logical reasoning as to why the student must remain in school. They do not see the current benefits of an education in a school that is directly related as a pathway to a future career for the student and their family.

Part of the reason for this presumption is the change in America's workforce. Now every teacher not only has to worry about teaching students and motivating them through the struggles of learning, but they must justify their teachings to all aspects of a student's life. Teachers move from being conveyors of knowledge to becoming the salesman trying to convince students to buy the product of education.

This new position did not happen just because of the COVID-19 pandemic but has slowly integrated into society. The latest pandemic has simply highlighted the disparity between education and its applicability to the world. The pandemic has also shed light on the seemingly true role of school, which is a place for students to be away from their parents. If a high school experience is going to really matter to the world, this perception must change. All aspects of a child's education must focus on a reason for them being in school.

The ultimate question is, "What is the purpose of a high school education?" The thoughts outlined in this book provide a pathway to that answer. Society must look at that question again and come up with a new answer for the new age of students. Unfortunately, the deciding bodies of the United States will probably not bring up this question. It is incumbent upon the educational society itself to redefine its role within the American society and declare its true purpose.

Enveloped within this new definition of school must be the flexible application of education to society's needs. The emergent reactions of education to the COVID-19 pandemic have shown that the institutions of education are not reliable and are very resistant to anything outside the normal process.

School districts were uncertain of exactly what to do with the lockdown situation that occurred during the initial phase of the pandemic. A shift to a virtual learning process was very challenging for all aspects of schools. Because there was no pre-planning of the situation, parents became distrustful of schools because they were not apprised of all the necessary decisions made for the situation. As this year of COVID-19 has continued, school districts are trying to wait out the situation in the hope that schooling will once again take the traditional model, thereby not having to change anything in the process. If this age of the pandemic comes to an end and there are no structural changes to the educational process, that will be a tragedy.

The irony of this entire situation is that learning in general is a flexible thing. Education can only be considered complete when the students completely master the skills that are outlined by the teacher. How that is taught is dependent upon the ability of the student to understand the learning. Therefore, all teachers must be as flexible as possible to ensure that students receive the necessary education for mastery. However, when it comes to the overall institution, this principle does not apply. It is a new time for education to become flexible.

That is not to say there were no successes. Innovative districts found a new capacity to adjust their learning in ways never before seen. The necessity of a virtual environment for teaching really showed the level of flexibility of teachers to adapt the learning to the situation. Some teachers were able to deal with the situation, others to thrive, and others found they became obsolete. Teachers who felt left behind have either left the profession or retired. For many teachers, the COVID-19 experience has reinvigorated the reasoning why teachers got into the profession in the first place. Many stories have continued to be shared of teachers truly desiring the established relationships they have always maintained and perpetuated. The concrete understanding of teachers changing lives is diminished in the virtual environment, and teachers long for that affirmation of their purpose within society. Most teachers have been able to accomplish this in some small way.

Initiatives outlined in this book are provided as a mixture of the current educational system and new methods that create more flexibility in teaching. The role of the teacher within the classroom will change because of the different aspects and focus that each teacher will provide to the classroom experience. The flexibility of tenured teachers' productivity within the educational institution will provide a structure where continual evolution of the teaching craft will be self-perpetuating. Utilizing the technology that has been learned in a dramatic fashion can now be leveraged to accelerate learning in a way never before seen. The creation of a multi-tiered school day that is understood by all stakeholders in a district can allow the flexibility of a district to implement any of these models, depending on what societal needs require. Imagine if these educational models had been understood and agreed upon prior to the pandemic. Additionally, who is to say there might not be another dire situation that would require education to have a similar reaction. The declaration, communication, implementation, and support during a shift could make the change seamless for everyone involved. This is the reason these ideas were offered.

By having schools focus on their prime directive for the purpose of every decision helps prevent future deviation from their sole purpose. The calendar and master schedule of any high school is not immune to this situation. Year-long course offerings provide a base where students, parents, and schools adapt the education to the needs of the students during their life. The educational experience becomes flexible to the student because the chosen number of educational segments allow the student to accelerate learning speed or decelerate for any unforeseen situation that might occur in a student's life. These school-year proposals allow the parents and students to declare the educational experience they see for their student. That is student-based learning.

It is understandable to be reluctant in implementing any of the ideas from this book. Leadership is always a difficult thing, which is why society admires leaders throughout all elements of society. The establishment of any of the measures outlined in this book will be a challenge for all aspects of the learning community. Everyone must be a part of the decision-making process and must be very clear on the motivations of *why* these things need to be done. The journey will be long and, in some cases, difficult.

However, most difficult journeys complete with the largest rewards. Our students deserve the best of every person within the educational community. They need nothing less than everything we can possibly create and implement. The darkest consequence of the COVID-19 pandemic on student learning is the despondency of students in thinking they cannot learn and that they are not smart enough to continue. This must stop. Implementing the measures outlined in this book can create a new day where the school sees its clear purpose, serves a clear purpose, is flexible in the implementation of that purpose, and creates a purposeful experience for every child.

Let us rise to this challenge and be as innovative as possible so our students can be the true future of American society.

References

Adams, C. (2009). The power of collaboration: Working with your colleagues can save you time and help you build a better classroom. *Instructor, 119*(1), 28-30.

Allen, T. C. (2013). *"Find the strength in every teacher": Urban middle school teachers' perceptions of effective change leadership* (Doctoral dissertation). Retrieved from ProQuest Dissertations and Theses database. (UMI No. 3571546)

Andrews, K. (2014). *Secondary language arts teachers' perceptions of the impact of school improvement grant professional learning communities on their professional practice* (Doctoral dissertation). Retrieved from ProQuest Dissertations and Theses database. (UMI No. 3626227)

Avolio, B. J., Zhu, W., Koh, W., & Bhatia, P. (2004). Transformational leadership and organizational commitment: Mediating role of psychological empowerment and moderating role of structural distance. *Journal of Organizational Behavior, 25*(8), 951-968.

Bass, B. M., & Riggio, R. E. (2006). *Transformational leadership*: Mahwah, N. J.: L. Erlbaum Associates, 2006. 2nd ed.

Bies, R. J., & Tripp, T. M. (1996). Beyond distrust: "Getting even" and the need for revenge. In R. M. Kramer & T. R. Tyler (Eds.), *Trust in organizations: Frontiers of theory and research.* (pp. 246-260). Thousand Oaks, CA: Sage.

Bloom, G., & Vitcov, B. (2010). PLCs: A cultural habit built on trust. *Leadership, 39*(4), 24-26.

Bretz, N. L. (2013). *Using professional learning communities to increase student achievement* (Doctoral dissertation). Retrieved from ProQuest Dissertations and Theses database. (UMI No. 3564167)

Brokaw, T. (2004). *The Greatest Generation.* United States: Random House.

Bryk, A. S., & Schneider, B. L. (2002). *Trust in schools: A core resource for improvement.* New York, NY: Russell Sage Foundation.

Burns, J. M. (2003). *Transforming leadership: a new pursuit of happiness.* New York: Atlantic Monthly Press.

Caine, G., & Caine, R. N. (2010). *Strengthening and enriching your professional learning community: The art of learning together.* Alexandria, VA: Association for Supervision and Curriculum Development.

Corcoran, T., & Silander, M. (2009). Instruction in high schools: The evidence and the challenge. *The Future of Children, 19*(1), 157-183.

Chu, L. (2017). *Little Soldiers: An American Boy, a Chinese School, and the Global Race to Achieve.* United States: Harper.

Cranston, J. (2011). Relational trust: The glue that binds a professional learning community. *Alberta Journal of Educational Research, 57*(1), 59-72.

Crowley, M. C. (Producer). (2019, March 09). Lead from the heart podcast [Audio podcast]. Retrieved from https://blubrry.com/ leadfromtheheartpodcast/42334779/amy–edmondson-why-psychological-safety-breeds-exceptionally-high-performing-teams/

Dalal, S. D. (2013). *Understanding how professional learning communities impact teaching practice and what influences the process* (Doctoral dissertation, Rutgers The State University of New York). Retrieved from https:// eric.ed.gov/?id=ED553292

Dever, R., & Lash, M. J. (2013). Using common planning time to foster professional learning: Researchers examine how a team of middle school teachers use common planning time to cultivate professional learning opportunities. *Middle School Journal, 45*(1), 12-17.

Doğan, S., & Yurtseven, N. (2018). Professional learning as a predictor for instructional quality: A secondary analysis of TALIS. *School Effectiveness and School Improvement, 29*(1), 64-90.

DuFour, R., DuFour, R., Eaker, R., & Many, T. (2010). *Learning by doing: A handbook for professional learning communities at work* (2nd ed.). Bloomington, IN: Solution Tree Press.

DuFour, R., & Eaker, R. (1998). *Professional learning communities at work: Best practices for enhancing student achievement.* Bloomington, IN: Solution Tree Press.

Dweck, C. S. (2006). *Mindset: The new psychology of success.* New York, NY: Random House Digital.

Eaker, R., DuFour, R., & Burnette, R. (2002). *Getting started: Reculturing schools to become professional learning communities.* Bloomington, IN: Solution Tree Press.

Edmondson, A. (1999). Psychological safety and learning behavior in work teams. *Administrative Science Quarterly, 44*(2), 350-383. doi. org/10.230 7/2666999

Edmondson, A. (2018). *The fearless organization: Creating psychological safety in the workplace for learning, innovation, and growth.* Hoboken, NJ: John Wiley & Sons.

Edmondson, A., & Lei, Z. (2014). Psychological safety: The history, renaissance, and future of an interpersonal construct. *Annual Review of Organizational Psychology and Organizational Behavior, 1,* 23-43. doi. org/10.1146/annurev-orgpsych-031413-091305

Escalante, D. (2019). *A mixed-methods study of how elementary principals build trust with staff using Weisman's five domains of trust model* (Doctoral dissertation). Retrieved from https://digitalcommons.brandman.edu/ edd_dissertations/238

Freire, P. (1990). *Pedagogy of the oppressed.* New York, NY: Continuum.

Goldman, S. G., & Pellegrino, J. W. (2015). Research on learning and instruction: Implications for curriculum, instruction, and assessment. *Policy Insights from the Behavioral and Brain Sciences, 2*(1), 33-41.

Gong, Y., Cheung, S.-Y., Wang, M., & Huang, J.-C. (2012). Unfolding the proactive process for creativity: Integration of the employee proactivity, information exchange, and psychological safety perspectives. *Journal of Management, 38*(5), 1611-1633.

Google. (2012). Guide: Understand team effectiveness Retrieved from https://rework.withgoogle.com/guides/understanding-team-effectiveness/steps/introduction/?gclid=EAIaIQobChMIoprR_4fO1gIVRIJ-Ch0AN-QjNEAAYASAAEgJaA_D_BwE

Gulbransen, M. A. (2016). *Exploring the strategic implementation of Common Core State Standards in small school districts of Northern California* (Doctoral dissertation). Retrieved from https://digitalcommons.brandman.edu/edd_dissertations/85

Gyesaw, S. (2012). *Teacher collaboration and collective efficacy in small learning communities (SLC) in urban high schools* (Doctoral dissertation). Retrieved from ProQuest Dissertations and Theses database. (UMI No. 3502221)

Hadar, L., & Brody, D. (2010). From isolation to symphonic harmony: Building a professional development community among teacher educators. *Teaching and Teacher Education, 26*(8), 1641-1651. doi.org/10.1016/j.tate.2010.06.015

Hargreaves, A., & Fink, D. (2006). Redistributed leadership for sustainable professional learning communities. *Journal of School Leadership, 16*(5), 550-565.

Hattie, J. (2012). *Visible learning for teachers: Maximizing impact on learning.* New York, NY: Routledge/Taylor & Francis Group.

Harvey, T. R., & Drolet, B. (2004). *Building teams, building people: Expanding the fifth resource* (2nd ed.). Lanham, MD: Rowman & Littlefield Education.

Hord, S. M. (2004). *Learning together, leading together: Changing schools through professional learning communities.* New York, NY: Teachers College Press.

Horn, I. S., Garner, B., Kane, B. D., & Brasel, J. (2017). A taxonomy of instructional learning opportunities in teachers' workgroup conversations. *Journal of Teacher Education, 68*(1), 41-54.

Howell, J. M., & Avolio, B. J. (1992). The ethics of charismatic leadership: submission or liberation? *Executive (19389779)*, *6*(2), 43-54. doi:10.5465/AME.1992.4274395

Hutt, G. K. (2007). *Experiential learning spaces: Hermetic transformational leadership for psychological safety, consciousness development and math anxiety related inferiority complex depotentiation* (Doctoral dissertation). Retrieved from ProQuest Dissertations and Theses database. (UMI No. 3262805)

Kanungo, R. N., & Mendonca, M. (1996). *Ethical dimensions of leadership*: Thousand Oaks [Calif.]: Sage Publications, c 1996.

Jackson, A. W., & Davis, G. A. (2000). *Turning points 2000: Educating adolescents in the 21st century.* Williston, VT: Teachers College Press. Retrieved from https://eric.ed.gov/?id=ED448910

Jones, J. E., & Bearley, W. L. (2001). Facilitating team development: A view from the field. *Group Facilitation, 3*(2), 56-64.

Joyce, B. (2004). How are professional learning communities created? History has a few messages. *The Phi Delta Kappan, 86*(1), 76-83.

Kimmons, R. (2016). Expansive openness in teacher practice. *Teachers College Record, 118*(9), 1-26.

Kolb, A. Y., & Kolb, D. A. (2017). Experiential learning theory as a guide for experiential educators in higher education. *Experiential Learning & Teaching in Higher Education (ELTHE): A Journal for Engaged Educators, 1*(1), 7-44.

Leban, W., & Zulauf, C. (2004). Linking emotional intelligence abilities and transformational leadership styles. *Leadership & Organization Development Journal, 25*(7), 554-564. doi:10.1108/01437730410561440

Lencioni, P. (2012). *The advantage: Why organizational health trumps everything else in business.* San Francisco, CA: Jossey-Bass.

Little, J. W. (2003). Inside teacher community: Representations of classroom practice. *Teachers College Record, 105*(6), 913-945.

Mertens, S. B., Anfara, V. A., Jr., Caskey, M. M., & Flowers, N. (Eds.). (2013). *Common planning time in middle level schools: Research studies from the MLER SIG's national project*. Charlotte, NC: Information Age.

Mitchell, R. M., Ripley, J., Adams, C., & Raju, D. (2011). Trust an essential ingredient in collaborative decision making. *Journal of School Public Relations, 32*(2), 145-170.

Moller, G. (2006). Teacher leadership emerges within professional learning communities. *Journal of School Leadership, 16*(5), 520-533.

Muhammad, A. (2009). *Transforming school culture: How to overcome staff division*. Solution Tree Press.

Mumford, M. D., Zaccaro, S. J., Harding, F. D., Jacobs, T. O., & Fleishman, E. A. (2000). Leadership Skills for a Changing World: Solving Complex Social Problems. *Leadership Quarterly, 11*(1), 11.

Muñoz, M. A., & Branham, K. E. (2016). Professional learning communities focusing on results and data-use to improve student learning: The right implementation matters. *Planning and Changing, 47*(1), 37-46.

Northouse, P. G. (2010). *Leadership : theory and practice*: Thousand Oaks: Sage Publications, c 2010. 5th ed.

Penuel, W. R., Fishman, B. J., Yamaguchi, R., & Gallagher, L. P. (2007). What makes professional development effective? Strategies that foster curriculum implementation. *American Educational Research Journal, 44*(4), 921-958.

Penuel, W. R., Frank, K. A., & Krause, A. (2006). The distribution of resources and expertise and the implementation of schoolwide reform initiatives. In S. A. Barab, K. E. Hay, & D. T. Hickey (Eds.), *Proceedings of the 7th International Conference of the Learning Sciences* (pp. 522-528). Mahwah, NJ: Lawrence Erlbaum Associates.

Peters, E. (2013). *Professional learning communities: Teachers' perceptions and student achievement* (Doctoral dissertation). Retrieved from ProQuest Dissertations and Theses database. (UMI No. 3558298)

Polhemus, C. E. (2010). *Collaborative behaviors among special education resource specialists, general education teachers, and their principals* (Doctoral dissertation). Retrieved from ProQuest Dissertations and Theses database. (UMI No. 3395317)

Raes, E., Decuyper, S., Lismont, B., Van den Bossche, P., Kyndt, E., Demeyere, S., & Dochy, F. (2013). Facilitating team learning through transformational leadership. *Instructional Science: An International Journal of the Learning Sciences, 41*(2), 287-305.

Schulte, M., Cohen, A. N., & Klein, K. J. (2012). The coevolution of network ties and perceptions of team psychological safety. *Organization Science, 23*(2), 1-18. doi.org/10. 1287/orsc.1100.0582

Senge, P. M., Cambron-McCabe, N., Lucas, T., Smith, B., & Dutton, J. (2012). *Schools that learn (updated and revised): A fifth discipline fieldbook for educators, parents, and everyone who cares about education.* New York, NY: Crown.

Sinek, S. (Writer). (2009). Start with why—how great leaders inspire action [Video file]. In *TedTAlks*. Puget Sound.

Sinek, S. (2011). *Start with why: how great leaders inspire everyone to take action*: Portfolio, Penguin.

Solomon, R. C., & Hanson, K. R. (1983). *Above the Bottom Line: An Introduction to Business Ethics*: Harcourt Brace Jovanovich.

Smith, H. H. R. (2015). *Development of trust and collaboration between teachers in PLC teams: The roles of teachers, principals and different facets of trust* (Doctoral dissertation). Retrieved from ProQuest Dissertations and Theses database. (UMI No. 3622127)

Szczesiul, S. A., & Huizenga, J. L. (2015). Bridging structure and agency: Exploring the role of teacher leadership in teacher collaboration. *Journal of School Leadership, 25*(2), 368-410.

Taylor, M. J. (2013). The benefits and drawbacks of common planning time for interdisciplinary team teachers: A new look in the era of No Child Left Behind. In S. B. Mertens, V. A. Anfara, Jr., M. M. Caskey, & N. Flowers (Eds.), *Common planning time in middle level schools: Research studies from the MLER SIG's national project* (pp. 109-130). Charlotte, NC: Information Age.

Tschannen-Moran, M. (2001). Collaboration and the need for trust. *Journal of Educational Administration, 39*(4), 308-331.

Tschannen-Moran, M. (2014). *Trust matters: Leadership for successful schools.* San Francisco, CA: Jossey-Bass.

Tschannen-Moran, M., & Hoy, W. (1998). Trust in schools: A conceptual and empirical analysis. *Journal of Educational Administration, 36*(3-4), 334-352.

U.S. Department of Education. (2010). *A blueprint for reform: The reauthorization of the Elementary and Secondary Education Act.* Retrieved from https://www2.ed.gov/policy/ elsec/leg/blueprint/blueprint.pdf

Wagner, T., Kegan, R., Lahey, L., Lemons, R. W., Garnier, J., Helsing, D., . . . Rasmussen, H. T. (2006). *Change leadership: A practical guide to transforming our schools.* San Francisco, CA: Jossey-Bass.

Weisman, M. (2010). *The process of measuring trust.* Santa Ana, CA: The Values.

Wicks, A. C., Berman, S. L., & Jones, T. M. (1999). The structure of optimal trust: Moral and strategic implications. *The Academy of Management Review, 24*(1), 99-116.

Made in the USA
Monee, IL
05 August 2021

74558663R10089